HOPE FOR RECOVERY

People don't realize the extent to which they're being controlled by their fear, guilt, shame, and compulsions. I know I didn't want to see these compulsions in myself, but they were there. I realized that my driving busy-ness to be enough, do enough, to please people, to fix *them* up in order to feel good about myself operated like any other addiction. But it wasn't until I followed the Twelve-Step program that I realized there was hope for recovery and that I could change my behavior. Let HOPE IN THE FAST LANE help you regain control of your life.

HOPE

IN THE FAST LANE

A New Look at Faith in a Compulsive World

Originally published
in a cloth edition as
*Sin: Overcoming the
Ultimate Deadly Addiction*

J. KEITH MILLER

HarperPaperbacks
A Division of HarperCollinsPublishers

HarperPaperbacks *A Division of* HarperCollins*Publishers*
10 East 53rd Street, New York, N.Y. 10022.

This title was originally published in a cloth edition as:
Sin: Overcoming the Ultimate Deadly Addiction.

A trade paperback edition of this book was published in 1990 by Harper & Row, Publishers, Inc.

First HarperPaperbacks printing: July 1991

Printed in the United States of America

HarperPaperbacks and colophon are trademarks of HarperCollins*Publishers*

10 9 8 7 6 5 4 3 2 1

To the bunch:

> Greg Burk
> Bill Cody
> Dan Henshaw
> Chuck Huffman
> George McGonigle
> Bob Slocum
> Roland Timberlake
> Paul Williams

with my love and gratitude

Acknowledgment

I am grateful to the authors and publishers mentioned in this book for permission to quote from their works. I have received ideas and help from many more people than I can acknowledge. I want to thank them all, and have tried to mention by name all those whose work and help were included consciously.

This project has been in progress for over two years. In many ways this has been the most difficult book I've ever tried to write. It has gone through several changes of content, direction, and title. I have wrestled with fear, discouragement, rejection, pain, shame, and joy as I have tried to deal with my own sin while writing about the disease sin spawned in the world. I almost gave up trying to describe denial. I realize its main characteristic is that people who have it don't know they do. And when some of those who first read my earlier attempts said they didn't know what I meant by denial, I was discouraged and wanted to quit. It almost seemed as if the Sin-disease didn't want a book written about it.

At various stages I asked people I consider good friends to talk to me about what I was trying to write, or to read all or parts of the manuscript. I know this took valuable time from their own lives, and I am more grateful than I can say to the following people who stood with me and helped in the creative process of getting this book completed:

Greg Burk, Bill Carter, Jim Colley, Fred Downing, Brooks Goldsmith, Richard Gorsuch, David Hardin, Howard and Carol Hovde, Chuck and Carolyn Huffman, Vester Hughes, Ann Hutchison, Earl Koile, Ron Land, Hugh Long, Ernie McAfee, and Scott Peck.

My editor and friend Roy M. Carlisle of Harper & Row, San Francisco, made some excellent structural suggestions that brought the book into focus for me and made it work. Lynn Williams gave me valuable editorial support and encouragement as she retyped and recopied the various versions over and over, especially during the past eighteen months.

My wife, Andrea—what can I say? Watching me struggle with my own sin as new aspects of it kept floating (or slithering) through the widening cracks in my denial couldn't have been all that much fun. But with remarkable frankness and love—and without getting sucked into my disease—she continued to give me the honest feedback I had to have to maintain my sanity and move ahead, personally and with the book. She taught me a great deal about healthy support with detachment and love.

To all these people I convey my love and gratitude.

Contents

V: Moving Beyond Ourselves

Foreword

It is with a sense of gratitude and some fear that I sit down to write these words. Since I was a small boy I have been on a search to understand how I might live and be happy in the face of the confusion and anxiety that plague my life and relationships. What is in this book represents the nearest I've found to an understanding of these problems and a way to live through them. At one level I had almost given up on ever finding any peace. And part of me is afraid to share what I am discovering for fear it will go away.

No book is for everyone. Some people may have their lives in good order and see a future of creative promise without serious conflict. They may have a great sense of serenity, clear communications with other people, and intimacy with those close to them and with God. I can rejoice about that.

This book is not for them. It is for those who have awakened lonely or frustrated in the night, anxious because, although they may be successful and even deeply religious, life and certain relationships in particular are confused, frightening, and threatening to overwhelm them, and they don't really know what to do. These people may have compulsive behaviors or thoughts they can't control. They may be secretly bored or turned off about faith or the church—or life itself. They are stressed and unhappy and don't know exactly why.

Sometimes such people have a vague and lonely anxiety, punctuated by growing periods of fear: fear about their future, about a child or other family member, about their sex life, some compulsive habit, their marriage—or lack of a marriage—or fear that they are "not going to make it" in a job or a relationship. The normal feelings of joy, pain, anger, fear, and guilt have often been repressed, giving such a person a kind of numb sense that he or she has life "under control." But from time to time (and more and more often) the feelings of fear, anger, and shame crop up in exaggerated forms, which tends to frighten and depress the person affected. For example, a mother may get absolutely *frantic* over a small daughter's not getting invited to a schoolmate's birthday party. Or a husband may become irrationally jealous and angry about a minor incident at a social gathering.

This book is written for anyone who has experienced some of the specific symptoms and general isolation I have described. Since the disease described here is spiritual in origin, and knowledge of it came to me through the Bible, I have used biblical references in describing sin throughout the book. And when sketching the history of sin I have talked about it in terms of my own spiritual heritage, which is Christian.

The disease, however, is not primarily a religious phenomenon but a *human* one. And the book is written to men and women of all religious preferences, or none at all, who struggle with misery and for happiness in their lives.

Because repression or denial is one of the primary symptoms, I could not hear or see my own diseased behavior for years, even though I was actively searching for anything wrong in my life so I could make it right. The people who finally helped me to see the marks of the disease in my behavior were those who were willing to reveal its *evidence* in theirs.

So the present investigation begins with something of my own encounter with the spiritual disease I've been discussing. In section three of the book I have included several chapters describing a way of living in recovery through which I am beginning to find a kind of sanity, serenity, and happiness I always knew must be out there somewhere.

Because of the personal revolution caused by my discovery of the Sin-disease and the denial and delusion in my own life, I have had to reevaluate all of my spiritual disciplines in order to try to stay in recovery from the Disease. A small part of the reoriented version of these disciplines in section III will be familiar to readers of my book *The Scent of Love*. But most of what is written here is part of what to me is a very different experience of trying to live in relationship to God.

I am aware that we are dealing with some of the basic mysteries of life here, and I have no illusion that I'm providing "definite answers" to such questions. Rather, this book is written in the spirit of sharing something of my own experience and hope as I wrestle with this spiritual malady while continuing to live in the contemporary fast lane. The pages that follow describe this "disease," its cause, and an approach to recovery from its pain.

J. Keith Miller
Austin, Texas

I
Source of the Problem

1

Attacked by a Strange Disease

I had been on the treadmill for twenty-one minutes
during my annual physical at the Houstonian Medical Center in Houston, Texas. I could feel the sweat
running down the back of my legs and hear my
breathing, which was labored but still steady and
strong. The muscles in my legs ached, but I had made
it for about twenty-six minutes the year before and I
was in great shape for a fifty-five-year-old—around
the ninety-ninth percentile, I had been told then—so
I felt confident that I'd make it to twenty-five or
twenty-six minutes again, although I was getting
pretty tired. The bundle of wires connected to my
heart contact points were cold when they brushed
against my stomach, but I was meditating to keep my
heart rate low, and my muscles relaxed as the elevated
treadmill motor droned on with its regular whirr-
chunk, whirr-chunk rhythm. My thoughts drifted to

the weekend before at the beach as I'd walked in the surf.

It was about nine in the evening. The moon was making a silver-orange highway to me across the blackness of the two-foot surf. I knew that something was really out of whack in my life. For years I had known, yet not quite been able to see, that there were things wrong inside me that I couldn't get a handle on. I had felt in my quieter moments that something bruised or broken inside my heart made me feel different from other people. I never seemed to belong— even though I appeared to be accepted and a part of things.

It was as if other people had been given a secret manual about how to get along and be loved and at home in life—and I hadn't got one. I'd always been lonely somehow and felt on the "outside." This outsider experience left me with feelings ranging from worrying vaguely about my life and close relationships to being half-crazy with anxiety about some financial problem, some issue relating to my own adequacy or success, or the welfare of one or another of my family members.

All my feelings seemed too big, and I tended to make crises out of small incidents. I had always assumed that such problems were "normal," but when I became a Christian I had been told that God promised to give us his peace, which would transcend the problems of the world. It was strongly suggested that our hearts don't have to be troubled or afraid. And when in my late twenties I made a serious commitment to become one of God's people, I was overjoyed to discover that I did find a happiness and peace that I had not known before. For several years I was an enthusiastic witness to the fact that God can and really does bring us some relief from our fears and anxieties.

In the years that followed I made a serious search for the meaning of life in light of the biblical faith. I wanted to know about God, and I wanted to find out how to live a sane and happy life. I have always been grateful for the love and acceptance I found and continue to find among God's people.

But as I walked along the beach that night kicking at shell fragments and sticks of silver driftwood I realized that I couldn't seem to stop taking on more commitments than I could handle. I'd become very lonely and separated from the people close to me— even though we were still speaking and relating to one another as usual, or almost as usual.

They had tried to tell me that I was working too hard. I thought they just didn't understand. Working hard has always made me feel fulfilled.

But my compulsive working no longer brought me the things I wanted. Instead, as the demands on me piled up, my attempts to "manage" the people close to me accelerated. I became more controlling and had more "suggestions" about how people should run their lives. I drank more wine before dinner, and during dinner, to "calm my nerves."

From my perspective, my family and business associates didn't respond the way I hoped. And they made what seemed to me to be unreasonable demands on me. Some of the close ones pointed to my "hidden" selfishness and made infuriating hints that I was not the hardworking, sensitive, and generous man I was trying to be. This made me very angry. I argued and justified myself and my actions at every turn with smooth explanations of my point of view.

These people didn't seem to appreciate how hard I was working for them. They didn't seem to understand the pressures in my life and work. I resented that and secretly blamed other people for the fact that I was not happy. I was bone-tired, but I couldn't seem to stop and rest from the all-encompassing busy-ness I had created with my compulsive behavior. I longed to do something just for me, but I had so many commitments I "had to meet" that there never seemed to be time for myself. The old standby I had always relied on—"when in doubt, work harder"—had backfired at last.

I tried to cut back on my activities. At first I was mildly surprised, then frightened, to see how difficult it was. After working all day I can remember saying when supper was over, "I think I'll work for about twenty minutes on this project. I have an idea I'd like to get on paper. Then we'll watch TV." Four hours later I'd look up and realize everyone had gone to bed.

Then one day I accepted a new commitment to do some very time-consuming projects—just as I had canceled some others because I had decided I was working too hard. I became angry when someone pointed out what I'd done. "That was an exception!" I snapped. But then I was afraid, because in my heart I knew it wasn't an exception. I was caught in the old compulsive trap of being overcommitted. I doggedly kept trying to reduce my work agenda to a manageable size so I could lead a sane, calm life. Before many months, however, I saw that I was powerless to change many of the compulsive ways I was living. And my fear grew to panic.

I began finding fault with my family, my publisher, the church, the IRS, my broker, and anyone else who "made unreasonable demands" on me or didn't see things the way I saw them. As a consequence I drove some people off and emotionally turned my back on others and walked away from them. Finally I was filled with feelings of self-pity, self-justification, self-righteousness, and myopic self-centeredness. Throughout this phase of my search for an answer, I kept my focus on what *they* were doing to *me*! I was miserable, and neither work nor prayer helped anymore.

I felt a heavy weight of sadness in my chest as I stopped and stared at the moon on the beach that night. Across the waves I could hear a familiar voice trying to ask me, "Do you want to stop?"

Through my reverie I heard the voice repeating itself. "Keith, do you want to stop? Do you want to get off the treadmill?" Dr. Don Wukasch was looking at the control board of the stress monitor. He had the moving cardiogram printout in his hand. "What?" I said.

"How are you feeling?" His voice was steady—too steady—and an alarm bell went off somewhere inside my head. I knew Don personally. We had codirected some conferences on "wholeness." I said, laughing, "Well, you might ask them to turn the air-conditioning down some. It's getting a little stuffy in here."

His reaction was completely unexpected. He turned quickly to the nurse and nodded. She began flipping the switches to turn off the treadmill. They told me to step carefully off the moving belt, and they led me across the small room to an examination table, where they suggested that I lie down. They were not smiling.

I laughed nervously, looking from one to the other, "Say, I wasn't finished, Don." But even as I said the words I had a sick feeling in my stomach as I looked at their faces. And I thought, "Oh, my gosh. Something's *really* wrong!" Suddenly I was afraid.

Don Wukasch, who had been a top surgeon on both Denton Cooley's and Michael De Bakey's heart teams, was in charge of the Houstonian at that time. In a few minutes, when my heart had gone back to a normal pattern, I said, "What's going on, Don?"

He looked at the printout. "Your heart has developed three different kinds of arrhythmias, and that combination is not good. There might be some serious blockage—and it ought to be checked. I've got a call in to a friend who's a cardiologist, and I want you to see him right away for some tests."

I was floored. I couldn't seem to grasp what he was saying—that it was about me. I'd always had a very healthy heart, had played basketball seriously for twenty years, and had a great physical fitness program. I felt a smothering wave of fear move into the room and drop on me like a cold, wet blanket. I was suddenly having trouble getting enough air, and I shivered as I felt the cold metal on the side of the examination table.

My wife, Andrea, was in the room by now. I didn't

know how much time had passed. "What do you do if there's blockage, Don?" I asked in a calm-sounding voice that I could hardly believe—considering the knot of fear that was now in the pit of my stomach. A picture of my own funeral had just flashed through my mind. I saw myself lying in an open casket. I looked down at my feet and shook my head to get rid of the casket picture. I noticed in a detached sort of way that my hands were sweating, and I automatically touched my temple with my index finger and noticed that it was damp too.

With a blue marker Don was drawing a sketch of a heart on the white drawing board built into the wall of the room. Like an anatomy professor he began to explain how the heart valves work, how the blood vessels and arteries could get clogged, and how bypass surgery worked. I felt light-headed and there was a nauseated feeling in my stomach. Andrea put a hand on Don's arm and nodded toward me. She said, "Don, I don't think Keith is as calm about this as you think he is." My face was evidently ashen, and I felt as though I was about to faint.

After a week of tests at Saint Luke's Hospital I found myself sitting across the desk from Don's cardiologist friend, who had routed me through the various tests for heart disease. The doctor was looking thoughtfully at the printout from the cardiogram taken during my stress test at the Houstonian.

"Mr. Miller, we don't know exactly what's wrong (and then he smiled) except that it isn't 'plumbing.' If you needed bypass surgery we could fix you up, and your chances of a complete recovery would be in the high nineties percentile range. But your problem seems to be more 'electrical' than 'plumbing.' And frankly, we don't yet know that much about curing this combination of electrical irregularities. When your heart is at rest it's almost normal." He continued, looking down at the printout and then back at me. "But make no mistake about this: if you don't change something in your life, this condition can kill you." His words echoed around the inside of my mind. "Kill you, kill you, KILL YOU!" As he finished speaking I suddenly knew what the problem was and what had happened. Smiling (rather grimly, I suspect), I said, pointing to the cardiogram, "Doctor, I know what those squiggly lines mean." He raised his eyebrows and looked at me. "What's that?"

"Doctor, that's a Morse code telegram from God telling me that my life's screwed up and I'd better get it straightened out."

His eyes narrowed and then he smiled and nodded his head. "Mr Miller, I think you're right"

I slipped into my planning mode and said, "Well, I've got four months to run on my commitment at the church, and I've got some speaking—" The doctor interrupted me with a very stern voice. "Mr. Miller, I don't think you're listening to me. If you want to get well, you need to change your life *now*! Or you may die."

We had moved to Houston only eight months before. The past two years had been a compulsive nightmare of work—almost all of which I had wanted to do and had volunteered for. How had I made things that complex?

I recalled that I'd been grateful when I'd decided to put my vocational lot in with God in 1962. I had become a speaker, conference director, and writer, and had thrown myself with abandon into communicating the good news about God that I was discovering. First I had become director of a conference center called Laity Lodge.

With some other people I had started several continuing small groups to support those who made new beginnings with God at the lodge conferences. These groups (ten at a time) met weekly in Kerrville, San Antonio, and Corpus Christi, Texas, which required a round trip of up to five hundred miles every week to each city. I was continuing to plan, recruit leaders and participants for, and direct weekend and weeklong conferences at Laity Lodge. In order to support people who became Christians at the conferences I would agree to pray for each of them by name for a month if they would pray for me. I knew how hard it was to change lifelong patterns alone.

This meant that each person who wanted to continue the specific prayer agreement had to write to me every month; I'd write a note back saying, "You're on for another month." At one time I had almost three hundred people I had been praying for (and corresponding with) personally. Besides this I was doing some speaking at conferences and conventions away from home about things that were happening through the community that was developing among those who had attended the conferences. When I looked back it was hard to imagine how I could have been so grandiose as to think I could do all those things. But I had felt I was doing God's will and had charged on.

Than I started writing, and after my first book (*The Taste of New Wine*) came out things really got wild. Letters came from everywhere, and I answered them all personally. People called for help at all hours, and I took the calls.

And now, sixteen years later, in Houston, in the months surrounding the physical, my work had become very stressful, and (I realized later) I had many of the classic signs of burnout. I had been codirecting conferences for executives and their wives at the Houstonian on physical, emotional, and financial wholeness. These conferences put people into active physical fitness programs, and I had bought the package. I was running several miles a day and doing strength-building weight exercises three times a week. Besides these regular activities I had written and been the sole speaker in six 45-minute movies on evangelism and one dramatic movie on Holy Week. I had written my tenth book and was writing another.

During this time I was a business consultant on retainer for a publishing company, and I had taken a job as a lecturer-in-residence at a large church in Houston, speaking twice a week and counseling on Mondays.

These things, plus my continuing correspondence and some independent business interests, finally had become too much. Yet I hadn't been able to see it. I just felt I needed to be better organized. But now, through my heart symptoms, God had finally got my attention. He was telling me in no uncertain terms that my life was out of control and I had to change if I wanted to continue living.

2

Out of the Stress Pool—A Slippery Bank

As I left his office the doctor told me that I was under a great deal of stress and overloaded and my only hope was to simplify my life. During the next few weeks I looked at what I was doing to see how much I could cut out. I was amazed to see what I have just told you. My life had become bizarre—and I hadn't even seen it. As a matter of fact, *no one* except Andrea had seen it all, because the people I worked with on different projects didn't know about each other. I would sometimes quit one activity temporarily while I charged into another. Although friends and family members had tried to tell me I was working too hard, somehow I had blinders on.

And now I really feared that I might die if I didn't cut the stress. So my wife and I set out to simplify our lives drastically in every way. First we made arrangements to move to Port Aransas, a small town on Mustang Island in the Gulf of Mexico, where we had a little beach house that was paid for. I quit my job at the church, and quit taking speaking engagements or doing conferences. Although I was afraid, I was also relieved. Something had stopped me at last, and now I was going to simplify after a lifetime of overworking. I felt a surge of hope.

Since I didn't know how long I might live, I began to get my financial affairs in order. I'd always been worried about money, but through some careless mishandling of my financial assets during my working binges, I had accumulated substantial debts. As I was in the process of analyzing my finances I got the idea that *that* was why I had always felt so inadequate and worked so hard—financial insecurity. If I got out of debt, my basic inner problem would be solved and I'd be serene.

So with a great deal of vigor Andrea and I made an action plan and began what turned out to be three and a half years of working to clear up all our debts and obligations. "*Then*," I thought, "I'll be at peace!"

So we cut our overhead, closed our office, operated out of our home, even sold one of our cars and bought two bicycles. The doctor had given me a diet to follow and a walking and jogging program that I really enjoyed and now had time for. I continued to work very hard, but it was like a vacation compared to what I'd done before. And I was justified now by the fact that I was at last on the way to whipping this strange, nagging inner sense of brokenness and lonely fear. (I know now that it sounds strange and irrational that I could think that getting out of debt would solve the deepest problem in my life, but that's what my mind fastened on—and I went for it.) My compulsive working was still there, but I didn't feel the effects of it so much because I was "getting my life cleared up" in the only area I could see that could be causing my anxiety.

Sure enough, three years later we were out of debt. We didn't owe money on house, car, or bicycle. I was free. My heart symptoms were gone—as if they had never been. I believed in God; my relationships with my family seemed to me to be good; I had health, no debts, and a vocation in which I had much experience. Now I was ready for the serenity and joy I'd worked so hard for all my life. On the day I realized I'd reached the goal of being out of debt I felt very tired but grateful. With God's and Andrea's help I'd solved my problem.

But that same evening after work, I felt worse than I had in many years. After supper I found myself anxious and sad, a tight band of fear around my chest and my mind filled with frantic negative pictures about the future. I saw myself as an old man alone and deserted. Who would want to live with a man who couldn't get his frantic life straightened out? I got up and went for another walk alone on a beach bathed in moonlight. I was really frightened now and shivered in the chill breeze coming across the water. I had all the things I'd always thought would make me happy, and I was miserable. Somewhere inside a small, quiet voice had kept telling me periodically that the real problem was something about *me* that I could not see.

But I'd ignored it and worked on. And now as I stood there in tears looking at the moon across the water it was as if a voice inside was telling me, "The time has come. You can't run anymore. You've got to face it." In that moment I realized that I was in the grip of a compulsive spiritual disease of some sort and that I was going to have to get outside help if I was ever going to find out what this cunning, baffling, and powerful force inside me was that was evidently out to kill me. It took the peace and enjoyment out of my life and yet hid from me so that I could not see it. I saw at last that I was truly powerless to fix myself alone and that even though everything "looked" all right, my spiritual and emotional life could no longer be fixed by financial security or any of the spiritual, medical, or psychological approaches I knew.

Finally, looking out across the night water and listening to the surf washing up at my feet, I turned to God once more as a frightened little boy. And I made a decision to go outside myself for help and counsel—whatever it took.

During the next two years I worked with counselors, groups, my minister, and my wife. As I got honest feedback from these people I began to discover a mystery about my own life, a mystery that had been hidden from me since childhood.

I saw that crouching behind my compulsive religious working and overachieving was a lonely and starved self, like a lost child—which in one sense I'd felt like all my life. That was true even though I had caring parents and a brother and we lived in a "Christian home." I saw that I was almost completely focused on getting love and attention. I used everything I had—all my talent and energy—to manipulate the people and things around me, often "for their own good," but really so they would love me and think I was a great person. I saw, in short, that I am an almost completely self-centered person, one who puts himself in the center and tries desperately to control his world and the people in it—traits I have always abhorred in other people. Since this had not been conscious, I'd never faced these behaviors and had built a life and a ministry trying to solve this need for feeling OK about me.

As I began to face myself at this new level I was horrified to see that this self-centered grandiosity, this playing God, I'd been involved in was "addictive." I could somehow hide it from myself, but despite all my resolve, I couldn't *stop* it. I realized that this compulsive, driving busy-ness to be enough, do enough, to please people (to get their attention, approval, or love), to fix *them* up in order to become OK myself, operated like any other addiction. There was in me an uncontrollable compulsion to repeat these self-defeating behaviors. Sometimes I felt as though I must be crazy not to be able to change simple habits I wanted to be rid of.

For example, I kept getting snarled up with people close to me. I would promise not to tell them what to do or try to run their lives. But then, *against my own will* it seemed, I would catch myself doing the very thing I had promised myself (and them) I would never do again. I was like a drug addict promising not to use chemicals and then going right back out and doing it. I could decide I was not going to give people close to me unsolicited advice or try to influence their decisions, yet at the end of every phone call or visit with certain people I would see that I'd done it again—and again. I could hear the anger and discouragement in their voices.

I discovered that I used work, intensity, alcohol, and religious activities to cover and blot out the feelings that would have revealed to me that though I might look like a humble fellow, I was playing God in people's lives to get the attention and approval I needed so desperately.

These may not seem like important issues to you, *unless* you have made resolutions—to change your eating habits, exercising habits, or drinking habits, to get rid of resentments or fears, or to *not* do things that are irritating to those around you. But I tried to change some of these things and was baffled when I could not. I saw that what I was doing was *sin* and I also saw that it was *addictive*.

Sin and Addiction—Blood Relations

It dawned on me with an awesome certainty that when people speak of themselves as being "sinners in need of God's healing" they are actually talking about being in the grips of the addictive spiritual disease that the Bible portrays in connection with "sin." I realized that this disease can disrupt our everyday lives and relationships and *never be seen to even be connected to sin.* And I saw that this Sin-disease may well be the matrix for all compulsive, manipulative, and controlling behavior. In an instant of clarity I saw that what we have always called sin just might be the source, the breeding ground, of all other addictions and for the irrational destructive and addictive behaviors that are destroying our lives and institutions across the world.

A Powerful Spiritual Approach

My counselor had told me that the best program ever devised for recovering from compulsive behaviors and addictions of any sort was the Twelve-Step program originally devised for alcoholics but now used by those addicted to food, people-pleasing, drugs, gambling, sex, religion, and many other things and relationships. I saw that I was compulsive in several areas.

As I began to take the simple steps I realized that here was a profound program of spiritual and physical healing that got at issues of spiritual sickness I had never been able to reach or even see through the traditional theological and psychological methods I had learned in seminary, in graduate courses in psychological counseling, and during over thirty years of studying the lives of the saints. Although those things had helped significantly and had led me to where I was, they did not deal directly with the repressed and compulsive behaviors of the Sin-disease I was now confronting.

After about a year of being in recovery I started to connect the sanity and security I was experiencing with the peace and joy that were such an integral part of the experience of the early Christian church.

I wondered if perhaps the simple spiritual program that was changing my life and the lives of thousands of people "right now" wasn't pretty close to the early church's clear recognition of sin and the gospel's remedy for it.

If this was true, then countless numbers of people might find their way to freedom . . . and to God.

3

A Brief History of Peace, Joy—and Sin—in the Church

Spiritual people of the biblical faiths believe that by surrendering themselves to God and trying to do his will, they will have freedom, peace, and joy in their lives.

As a believer in the God of Jesus Christ, I had often heard this. In fact, from the first vibrant words of the New Testament I sensed that there was an aura of joy and freedom from bondage that the writers were obviously experiencing through their faith in God. Although I didn't doubt their experience, I began to suspect that there was something they were doing that we don't know about now. I recalled that after each of my own attempts to "give it all to God," I experienced for a while what I thought was the joy and peace the New Testament writers pointed to. I'd wake up in the morning and smell the earth after a spring rain. I'd feel so forgiven and accepted that I would think God had freed me from my "bondage" to defensive reactions and compulsive panic about my financial future. But it wouldn't be long before I was again anxious, frustrated, and lonely, even though I was doing the Bible study, worship, and witnessing that other Christians told me was the way to live for Christ.

I began to wonder what had happened to those freeing and life-enhancing aspects of experience in the church. Was the joy the early believers wrote about a gift from God that caused them to live differently; or did they work out a different way to live that led to peace and joy?

I asked questions: Are happiness and freedom from compulsive worry and frustration really possible for thinking, growing people who face the risk and change of today's fast lane? Or are they myths unconsciously passed on by pious Christians to falsely encourage commitment and devotion among the unsophisticated?

Finally I concluded that the joy and calm contentment contemporary Christians talked about was not real—after the first few years. I decided that the continuing peace and joy the saints spoke of was an exaggeration, or at least something that didn't apply to people like me who were in business, raising families, and traveling in the twentieth century. I decided to review the church's history to try to find out what had happened. But then, through a series of discoveries and crises in my own life, which I discuss in this book, I made some radical adjustments that have turned my world upside down and changed my mind about the possibility of serenity in the midst of life.

The Problem of Sin: A Review of What May Have Happened to Freedom, Peace, and Joy

When Jesus came two thousand years ago the Roman world was a scary place. Life was physically brutal and dangerous for subject peoples like the Hebrews. One had to be careful not to irritate the conquerors.

Within the Jewish community there had always been the twin swords of guilt and swift punishment by God for those who had sinned against his law. Since potentially that included everyone, a lot of care was taken by religious people to avoid sinful acts. If "sins" were committed, the sinner had to go through ritualized sacrificial processes to get back to a right relationship with God, with the person sinned against, and with the Jewish community.

This was serious business, because punishment for sins could be exclusion from the community or even death. Only those who were in a status of righteousness could hope for the *shalom* (peace, health, and joy) of God.

So when Jesus came and announced forgiveness for all sins and even a victory over death for those who repented, confessed, and surrendered their lives to God, there was an outbreaking of personal freedom and joy among those who responded—even in the face of martyrdom. This uncanny exuberance and serenity were essential marks of the new Christian family as they gave each other—and even their enemies—the love they were receiving. They were no longer afraid of either the Romans or the Law.

The New Way of Dealing with Sin

Because of the people's fear of God and the stark reality of punishment, sin had been one of the most important issues of life, and *the* most important *problem* for many religious Jews. Without dealing with sin there could be no peace and joy, only guilt and the fear of discovery and punishment.

So, although the Jewish sacrificial system was no longer binding for Christians, it was not unusual for early Christian meetings to reflect the importance of dealing with sins specifically and openly. But the surprising thing to me as I looked back at the early church was the *life-and-death* importance they placed on rigorous honesty in confronting sins. In Acts 5 is the account of two members of the early church who had lied about how much money they had received for a piece of property. They had "held out" on God and the community. When they were confronted they were both stricken, "fell down and died," in the presence of Peter.

This focus on dealing openly with people's sins in the fellowship after conversion continued as little groups of Christians were planted and took root throughout the Roman world:

The early Christian church cells were comprised of small groups of people who met regularly—often secretly. The order of worship was, first of all, self-disclosure and confession of sin, called *exomologesis*. This was followed by appropriate announcement of penance, pleas for forgiveness, and plans for making restitution. A final period of friendly fellowship (*koinonia*) closed the meeting.[1]

The process of specifically searching out thoughts and acts of disobedience to God has continued to be crucial for many Christians. Confession has been the broom to sweep clean the communication channel to God through which he sends back his freedom, peace, and joy.[2]

What the Gospel Solved in the "Here and Now" of Life

Behind the gospel message was a universal dilemma that has plagued men and women from the beginning: in human nature and experience there is a basic inner conflict. There is something "broken" that cannot be "fixed," something wrong that cannot be corrected by all the success, effort, money, pleasure, power, or ability in the world. There is a basic fear, an aching pain and frustration in life, that cannot be covered up forever by smiles and outward trappings of success.

Sooner or later a lonely anxiety breaks out and spreads like a poisonous gas to every corner of our lives. We sense that all we own or have accomplished is no longer important if we can't feel the peace of knowing that we are "all right" in a real and continuing way. Yet at times we feel that we never will be. We seem to be separated from that worthiness we long for, from other people and from God. Compulsively we dash off in all directions to try to "feel better," to avoid those frightening and painful feelings we fear may overwhelm us.

Men and women in this condition have always cried out, "How can I get rid of my haunting, lonely feelings of separation and unworthiness?" The question is as old as humanity and as broad as the world. We are somehow "wrong" and want to be made "right." There's a tragic disharmony in the experience of life that cries out to heaven itself for adjustment. We feel that we are "supposed" to be happy and free, yet we feel anxious and not free. The Genesis story says that our separation was a part of the experience of the first man and woman (Gen. 2:15–3:24). But all men and women since seem to need to be reconciled to Something. And the Old Testament looked for God to come himself and make things right.

Finally, the gospel arrived and promised that God would overcome the separation if people would commit their lives to him as they saw him in Jesus. Many did, and they felt the release and subsequent freedom, peace, and joy in his kingdom. As the author of Colossians said, "He has delivered us from the dominion of darkness and transferred us to the kingdom of his beloved Son, in whom we have redemption, the forgiveness of sins" (Col. 1:13–14). And Paul said that this kingdom is "righteousness and peace and joy in the Holy Spirit" (Rom. 14:17).

What Happened After the Surrender

But there was a problem. After the surrender, the anxiety and separation came back—again and again.

And the church evidently discovered that only when Christians kept facing squarely the specific behaviors their sin caused, repented, confessed them openly in the Christian community, asked for forgiveness, and made amends in every way possible could they receive the healing forgiveness they continued to need. Through this process, God kept washing the sins from people's minds, in the same way you would clean a blackboard.

What followed this act of claiming moral responsibility for one's sins by confessing and dealing with them specifically was joy and peace or serenity. The inner conflict was over, and forgiven Christians were acceptable to God, to their brothers and sisters in Christ, and to themselves. They didn't have to run compulsively from their sins and fear and pain. They had confessed them and received God's forgiveness and the love of the community. They were free to breathe deeply, to live and love again for another day.

The happiness was amazing. Many people had never experienced it. But like the manna in the wilderness, it could be acquired only "one day at a time." And the regular and continuing process of dealing with sins and character defects, the process that renewed the peace and joy, seems to have been crucial.

All this discovery and confession of sins took place among Christians after the initial commitment to God in the fellowship of those who were surrendering to him.

The "Sin" Behind the "sins"

Since dealing specifically with one's sins became the basic therapy the church had for its members and the world, it was very important to decide what constituted sin.

Many have always thought that the specific sinful acts are what constitute sin (e.g., murder, rape, theft). But theologians like William Temple believed that those specific sinful acts that propel us back into the state of guilty brokenness from which life has no remedy (apart from God) are only symptoms. They are symptoms of a basic and all-encompassing self-centeredness, a need to control in order to get what we want, an attitude that colors every relationship, and emasculates the one with God. It is this deeper, more central attitude that leads to all the thoughts and actions we call sins. And it is the underlying attitude that is *Sin* (with a capital *S*).[3]

At various times in history this basic Sin has been conceived of as rebellion against God, estrangement, isolation from the community, lack of trust, or error in performance ("a missing of the mark"—the old Greek meaning). But as used in the present context these words reflect defiant withdrawal and self-absorption. William Temple said,

There is only one Sin, and it is characteristic of the whole world. It is the self will which prefers "my" way to God's—which puts "me" in the center where only God is [should be] in place.[4]

Sin, in this view, is about our apparent inability to say no to our need to control people, places, and things in order to implement our own self-centered desires. We do this either with blatant power or through apparent weakness—for example, by taking care of people but making a thousand minute suggestions about how they should run their lives. We may believe in God and love him a great deal, but at the essential level *we* are in control—or struggling to be.

A Road Back to Freedom, Peace, and Joy

In the early church it was this deep underlying Sin (which kept revealing itself in specific sins) that had to be dealt with before there could be any serenity among God's people.

The initial surrender the early Christians made to God dealt with their powerlessness to overcome Sin alone or through the law. This commitment and baptism constituted an identification with God's ultimate victory over Sin and death. After conversion they found they could then use the power of God to overcome particular sins that continued compulsively to plague them and destroy their relationships. When a Christian put him or herself in the number-one position and became separated from God and other persons by self-centered thoughts and deeds, the old guilt and lonely anxiety would threaten to overcome that person again until he or she dealt with the specific sins. Then the freedom, joy, and peace of God returned.

This was where the undeserved love and forgiving grace of God met Christians at their deepest point of need: their guilt, fear, and broken relationships caused by Sin.

The Protestant Reformers

The Protestant Reformers objected to what they considered to be the Roman church's "selling" certain aspects of this gift of forgiveness and serenity. To them, paying money for indulgences that "bought" forgiveness in the confession process adulterated the confessional, and in fact the Roman Catholic church changed these practices during its own time of reform.

Because it was so important an issue during the Reformation, some Protestants believe that Luther and Calvin wanted to do away with "confession," but that is not true. They only wanted to stop the abuses of their time. Both Luther and Calvin were in favor of the act of confession; Luther said that confession

is useful, even necessary, and I would not have it abolished. Indeed, I rejoice that it exists in the church of Christ, for it is a cure without equal for distressed consciences. For when we have laid bare our consciences to a brother and privately made known to Him the evil that lurked within, we receive from our brother's lips the word of comfort spoken by God Himself. And if we accept this in faith, we find peace in the mercy of God speaking to us through our brother.[5]

The Lutheran and Reformed churches attempted to restore the ancient public penitence of the early church.[6]

But evidently the alleged abuse of the practice of confession and penance, along with Luther's cry that grace through faith alone was all that was necessary, caused the practice of confession to decline among Protestant Christians.

However, when the church has neglected the healing confession-forgiveness process, either rigid legalism or spiritual apathy have often been the result— only to be shattered periodically by renewal movements in which the continual surrender to God and the facing and confession of sins are central. These renewal movements have been characterized by a release of freedom, joy, and hope. For example, the weekly public confession of the Wesleyan cell groups in the eighteenth century had much of the flavor of the confessional meetings of the early church.

This specific confession of sins to God before other Christians was *not* a punishment. On the contrary, it was a gift, the only doorway in the world through which a person could walk to find freedom, peace, joy, and healing for his or her deepest recurring pain and anxiety.

People have always been baffled by the necessity for the unrelenting warfare against Sin in the world. "Why isn't *one* confession enough?" they cry. But it is as if Sin forced people to repeat compulsively those very self-centered behaviors that made them miserable. The process of confession freed them to face and even overcome the recurring behaviors and the character problems that caused them. As Luther's comment implies, dealing with sins confessionally is tied to a healing peace, joy, and security of life.

But history seemed to conspire against the continuance of this great blessing of the good news.

4

The Effects of
Excessive Zeal,
Science, Medicine,
and Secularization

Over the years several things supported the decline of the process of repentance—confession—forgiveness—restitution—and its resulting serenity.

Excessive Zeal

For one thing, the importance of the status of righteousness was so central to the Christian enterprise that the punishments meted out by the church for sinning were very severe. Somehow the keepers of the kingdom seemed to "forget" the grace-filled aspect of the gospel. Many Old Testament practices continued.

Children were whipped regularly by "good Christian parents" to "keep them" from Sin. The Scriptures were used to back up this practice; "He who spares the rod hates his son" (Prov. 13:14) and "If you beat him with the rod you will save his life from Sheol" (Prov. 23:14).

In the Christian community adults were stoned to death for certain sins. In alter times people were put in stocks and had their tongues slit for such things as gossiping, stealing, and practicing witchcraft. The punishment often became more abusive than the crime. Since kings usually were believed to rule by divine appointment, they could devise whatever punishments they thought appropriate for crimes. Sins were still under the umbrella of God's authority, but then kings were his servants.

Secularization of Punishment

After the reign of Henry VIII in England many sinful acts became not only immoral but illegal (murder, mayhem, robbery, treason, and scores of others, each with specific punishments). Since the government took over punishment for these, the churches were left basically the seven cardinal sins to deal with (anger, greed, pride, sloth, envy, lust, and gluttony).[1]

As history continued and a middle class developed, government took on more definition, and the function of dealing with certain sins gradually left the hands of the church and went to the secular courts in more and more countries. Serious social sins were called "crimes." And the church was often left to deal with sins that were considered dangerous to the *spiritual* welfare of the people—or the church. Since this was an arbitrary classification, what a sin was could vary a lot. Torture was used, and many were burned at the stake or subjected to humiliating public penance.[2]

In modern times Sin finally became a personal matter between an individual and God and was most often dealt with privately within the church membership—though in some cases punishments were still severe. In the United States the law went into fine moral detail (e.g., in Connecticut doing laundry on Sunday or using profanity in the presence of the mayor was illegal).[3]

Science and Medicine

The ascendancy of science and medicine exposed some of the penitential practices and beliefs of the church as primitive, abusive, and irrational. And the church's history of excessive punishments for sins was condemned.

With Freud's discovery of the unconscious mind and his mechanistic view of the psychic processes it began to be assumed that much that had been labeled and punished as "sin" was not really the fault of the sinner, but arose out of faulty relationships with his or her parents. Many antisocial behaviors that had been called sins were labeled illness. Words like *bad* and *wicked* began to seem old-fashioned when seen through the lenses of some schools of psychology. Both sins and crimes had come under the umbrella of "illness" and "symptom;" and many abuses were curbed by these developments.

A few sins remained in the church (e.g., hating a brother, dishonoring one's parents, adultery, or blaspheming the Holy Ghost), but even these were sometimes explained away by psychological theories. To call these things sins wasn't useful anymore. Finally the only sin that seemed left for the church to deal with was that of alienating God.

The Church's Reaction

In reaction to science's discoveries and "sin-free" philosophies, some conservative Christian groups went in the opposite direction. They focused on sins and threat of eternal punishment (damnation) with a grim and renewed vigor, sometimes seemingly to the exclusion of the gospel's message of love, grace, and creative freedom. But although the public condemnation of sins was a major thrust in these churches, the remedy of open confession to each other (or private confession to a minister), forgiveness, and restitution was not a part of most conservative Protestant church life—especially *after* the initial conversion and forgiveness. The rationale for abandoning private confession to a minister lay in the misconception some had that the one in whose presence the sinner was confessing was acting as an intermediary. "We do not need intermediaries. We go directly to God," some conservative Christians argued.

By contrast, many of the more liberal-minded churches had followed the practitioners of secular science and medicine who, with their rational theories (and their horror at the brutality and vengeance they saw that was masked as righteous punishment), had rejected the whole notion of Sin. As "science" entered the theological scene in the demythologizing of the Bible, there was a great wave of uncertainty in mainline churches concerning which of their beliefs and practices were still valid in light of new discoveries.

In this moment of doubt mainline churches often went with the intellectual mainstream. Dealing with Sin and the confession-forgiveness process was effectively eliminated in the Protestant church at large.

In both liberal and conservative churches the original notion of public confession of sins in a Christian group often came to be thought of as archaic, naive, embarrassing, or dangerous.

But "Progress" Left a Terrible Void

But there was a problem: the new discoveries of science didn't take into consideration the age-old fact of every person's most basic dilemma—that in human nature and experience there is something "broken" that cannot be "fixed" (even with all the pills and skills of modern medicine), something wrong that cannot be made right by all the success, money, power, or even knowledge one can gain or all the psychotherapy one can go through.

And there were moral and psychological consequences to eliminating Sin from society's agenda.

In 1972 Karl Menniger wrote a book called *Whatever Became of Sin?* in which he raised some serious questions about the moral condition of a people who could dismiss the concept of Sin. But although the book was widely read no one seemed to pick up on the themes Menniger presented.

At about the same time the historian Arnold Toynbee pointed out that

> science has . . . also begun to find out how to cure psychic sickness. So far, however, science has shown no signs that it is going to be able to cope with man's most serious problems. It has not been able to do anything to cure man of his sinfulness and his sense of insecurity, or to avert the painfulness of failure and the dread of death. Above all, it has not helped him to break out of the prison of his inborn self-centeredness into communion or union with some reality that is greater, more important, more valuable, and more lasting than the individual self.[4]

In short, the basic sense of separation, called Sin, that has caused people to cry out to God from the beginning of history is still with us. Unwittingly we did a terrible thing in the name of enlightenment. We virtually eliminated the gospel's healing process for recovering from the continuing and addictive effects of Sin. In removing Sin and its remedy from the church's life, we seem to have lost the gifts of freedom, happiness, and serenity.

In Mainline Churches

Some sad things happened in churches that separated themselves from the Sin-confession-forgiveness process that relieves people's greatest anxiety and loneliness.

In churches I attended early in my Christian life there appeared to be little of the passionate evangelism and sharing that comes as a response to the joy experienced by the forgiven Christian continually being made new.

I remember an older woman in our town who babysat for a living. She seemed to be unusually happy and peaceful. She was open, generous, and loving to everyone. I remember grown Christians shaking their heads in embarrassment when she spoke about how much she "loved Jesus" because he had forgiven her. Once she brought a whole row of people to church. And although no one could knock that sort of behavior publicly, I made a mental note that one shouldn't do that if one wanted to be accepted socially in our church. The loving forgiveness of God for Sin was not an "in" thing to discuss.

Some mainline churches became disconnected liturgical stations, somber study groups, or boring lecture halls dealing with sociological and theological problems.

In these churches, committees worked hard behind the scenes to dream up programs that would "interest the unchurched." I worked on some of these. And I can remember being bored out of my skull with some of the theoretical programs we devised for people who, from all outward signs, had not even thought about turning their lives over to God. I remember that we had one program that required up to several hours preparation a week and dealt with the liturgy of the church from a historical perspective. At least I *think* that's what it dealt with. It was so uninteresting to me as a person trying to find out who God was and what he wanted me to do with my life that I can't remember the exact content. But I do remember that the course was impersonal and dry and unrelated to the nuts and bolts of my life. And I was supposedly pushing the course. The programs were designed to bring new people in and help them grow. But I attended several churches in which the whole enterprise was often only marginally relevant to my real life and relationships, which were snarled up by compulsive resentments, fears, and other Sin-caused character defects.

Everywhere I looked the anxiety and loneliness were like an epidemic spiritual constipation blocking the joy and serenity that, I now realize, could have come from confession and forgiveness.

Evangelical Churches

During all this time many of the churches that appeared to grow and flourish did focus on the basic gospel message that we are all separated form God, all sinners. They announced the good news that if we will commit our lives to Jesus Christ we will find hope, immediate forgiveness, meaning, and eternal salvation.

Although I wasn't raised in an evangelical church, there came a time as an adult when I realized I needed to commit my life to God and his cause and made a beginning commitment. After I made this first surrender of my life to God, I experienced a sense of freedom, exhilaration, and rightness about myself. Later I was told that that experience was my conversion. And my life really did change in almost every area. But the trouble was that, after a few glorious years of witnessing and writing about the faith, I found many of my old habits and behaviors had *not* been dealt with and healed—even though I prayed about them every day.

Now, looking back, I can see that many of us caught up in the evangelical renewal were never taught the process of dealing with our continuing sins, the process that begins on *this* side of that first commitment and surrender. Having done away with the repentance, confession, forgiveness, and restitution *after* conversion, evangelicals had no process or liturgy in the community of faith to which they might take this postbaptismal anxiety and guilt for healing. There was little calm contentment or joy after the "conversion honeymoon" wore off.

We were baffled, since our faith commitment was still in place. We had sincerely done what we thought was necessary to put God in the center of our lives and be healed of our "brokenness that cannot be fixed." But we didn't feel healed. I remember an older minister sitting on a hillside at a conference center one summer telling me that I was naive to think the freedom and continuing happiness would remain after the initial honeymoon period was over. I didn't believe him, but I didn't know why I wasn't joyful and free anymore.

It wasn't that we were consciously being dishonest. We weren't most of the time. If we thought about it at all, we just felt that something about our faith was not as "strong" as it used to be. But we felt anxious and restless and a little guilty.

In order to keep any semblance of freedom, joy, and gladness—which we rightly saw as the marks of a seriously committed Christian—we had to do two things: we had to have continual evangelistic meetings where enthusiasm and exuberant happiness flowed into the group through the lives of the newly converted. We had to learn to hide from ourselves and other people the sins we continued to commit and the anxiety and separation we continued to experience in our own lives. For many of us this meant continuing to talk about the joy and peace of Christ long after these things had slipped away and our hearts had little more than a memory of them. The distance between our true and often uncomfortable inner experience and our victorious public professions was a silent scandal of unreality that made authentic confession and forgiveness more and more difficult in many gospel-preaching evangelical churches.

Since much of this was *not conscious,* and no one talked about it, many of us were unaware that we had drifted from the inner happiness and serenity of God. And many of us did *not* connect what was happening inside us at a feeling level to our faith—since we still believed strongly.

Sin Has Power and Energy of Its Own

As I have just tried to show, Sin had gotten itself eliminated from the agenda of Christians after they were in the fold. There is a strong implication that once a person is converted, Christ has "taken away Sin," and the person is free and doesn't need further confession, forgiveness, and restitution. Yet many of us in and out of the church are suffering from a spiritual disease, the symptoms of which look a lot like products of "preferring our way to God's" and "putting ourselves in the center where only God belongs." We are self-centered even in our "Christian lives," and we have lost the selfless love and the joy and gladness of the good news. In fact, although it is seldom discussed, many of us seem to be eaten up with the Sin-disease of hidden selfishness.

But try as we will to ignore Sin, we do not take into account that Sin has always had a kind of destructive and compulsive (addictive) energy of its own. We ignore the fact that

> our age is as haunted by sin as any other—perhaps more so—the problem of sin is the axial problem of human thought and no effort of man's mind has any lasting importance that is not concerned with that problem.[5]

There is a frightening and tenacious quality about this deeply embedded tendency to put ourselves in the center and try to get our own way. It seems to defy the most powerful efforts of our human will to change it. For example, I can remember a bewildered woman coming to me and saying, "I don't understand what's happening. After becoming a serious Christian I felt free of resentment; for a while I loved everyone. Since I had committed my life to Christ I felt sure that I had been healed forever from resentment of a cousin. This cousin used to do some things that before my conversion irritated me almost daily, and I would resent her continually. But recently when she was to come for visit I vowed that I would remember my commitment to God not to resent her, and I asked God for his help.

"I promised God that I would not resent this woman, repeating to myself, with all sincerity, 'I will *not* resent her. I will *not* resent her. I will *not* resent her!' But when she walked in my front door and said, 'Hello,' I was suddenly *filled* with resentment. I was baffled. I saw that I had wanted her to be different, and she *wasn't*. I hadn't meant to resent her. I was like an alcoholic promising not to drink. I wanted to change my behavior, but I seemed to be in the grip of a strange compulsion to try to get this cousin—and everyone else—to be the way I wanted them to be."

As I thought about what this woman had said a light went on in my head. I saw that the tenacity and compulsive nature of Sin in my life acts very much like the compulsive drivenness of a person who is addicted to a chemical. And if it was true that Sin does in fact behave as an addiction that has us Christians caught in its web, then that might explain the baffling compulsive nature of Sin in our lives. Perhaps seeing it that way could help us come to grips with our own Sin and find a way to recovery.

5

The Relation of Addiction to Sin

When many of us think of an addict we think of a tattered drunk lying under a bridge with an empty green wine bottle clutched to his chest. And it is true that the idea of addiction and addictive traits first came to be studied because of the destructive and progressively diseased behavior of people who were seemingly bonded to chemical substances. Those who were "addicted" continued to use these chemicals even though it was apparent to others that their use led to broken relationships, loss of the ability to use natural talents, physical and emotional separation from their morals and highest ideals, and finally physical disease and even death. Their craving was eventually totally uncontrollable. People in the grips of a chemical addiction could be brilliant doctors, statesmen, psychiatrists, religious leaders. They could understand with their minds that continued use of the chemical agent would lead them to emotional, spiritual, and physical ruin. Still they would not (could not) stop the addictive behavior.

When chemical addiction began to be recognized as a major social problem, especially after the Second World War, science began to study addictions with more intensity.

An Underlying Disease

What the researchers have discovered is that there is, beneath the chemical usage, and separable from it, an elusive underlying dynamic. There is something that operates like a disease that can fasten the patient's attention compulsively on many different things. As L. J. Hatterer said, "The word 'addicted' has become generalized and is no longer confined to the World Health Organization's definition [which only describes addiction to drugs].... In common parlance addiction relates to any substance, activity, or interaction."[1] In other words, people are now seen to be "addicted" to such different things as food, smoking, gambling, work, spending money, play, video games, sex, pleasing people, and religion. As Harvey Milkman and Howard Shaffer stated in their book *The Addictions*, "Alcoholism is only one of multiple patterns of expression for addictive disease."[2] Like cancer, addiction is a basic, primary disease, and it expresses itself through various chemicals and behaviors. It's as if beneath the addictive behaviors there is some unseen cause in the life of the addicted person; it is this underlying cause that is the real root cause. The alcohol or other addictive agents or behaviors are the ways thin underlying cause expresses itself in the outer life of the addict, symptoms of the underlying illness and not the illness itself.

The Payoff and Underlying Purpose

The individual who is in the addictive process has a strong conscious desire or need for a substance, object, action or interaction, fantasy, and/or atmosphere that produces a mental/physical high. This is the conscious payoff of the addictive behavior. This desire or need repeats itself and is impulsive and compulsive in nature. The (often unconscious) purpose of the high is to ease or blot out any physical or psychic discomfort, conflict, pressure, stress, or pain (that may be caused by the basic underlying disease). For example, if a man is addicted to work, when he is beginning to worry inordinately about control of financial matters or have feelings of anger (or inadequacy) in his marriage, he may begin compulsively working late at night and on weekends, even if he isn't required to. The compulsive working will ease the immediate fear he is facing. A person whose addictive choice is alcohol would "have a couple of drinks" or decide to "have a party" to cover his or her fear or pain. And so on.

At first the addiction "works," since the one working or drinking, for example, gets a kind of euphoric high that is a relief from the unpleasant feeling about to surface. But as time goes on, the high diminishes. The addict obtains progressively less relief for the same amount of alcohol or work. Finally, the person enters a painful depressed state called withdrawal whenever he or she is not engaging in the addictive behavior. Ultimately the addictive behavior brings no relief, no blotting out or coping with the pain, and only very slight pleasure, if any. Yet the addict finds that he or she cannot stop the drinking or working—even if it becomes apparent that it will lead to serious physical symptoms, even death. Even long after the addictive agent has quit working, there is an irrational hope that "this time" it will work again and relieve the haunting sense of worthlessness and fear.

At this point tension, anxiety, depression, guilt (for neglecting and/or abusing those nearby with the extremely self-centered behavior that goes with any addiction) may increase. Paranoid reactions, fear, mood swings, and/or physical changes and deterioration of life-style may lead to destructive confrontations in one's intimate relationships, as well as the increased neglect and physical absence caused by the addictive agent or behavior.

Chief Characteristic: Denial

Perhaps the chief characteristic of addiction is "denial," by which the individual is blinded to the extent of the addictive behavior in his or her life. Denial is a form of repression through which people blot out certain aspects of their own behavior *from their own view*. For example, a man who is an alcoholic and has been roaring drunk for two days may say, and *honestly believe*, that he has "just had a couple of drinks." The work addict says, and often believes, that he or she is just working extra hard *temporarily*—"until this project (week, year, merger, etc.) is completed." Living in the delusion caused by denial, such a person creates a rationale that justifies all of the addictive behaviors as being necessary, right, or even unselfish. There is an intense need in the addict to be seen as "right" or perfect. Any criticism or indication that one's behavior is less than perfect and right is often met with intense anger and/or defensiveness and elaborate self-justi- fication.

Character defects such as dishonesty, manipulation, gossiping, blaming others, insatiability (with regard to attention, money, power, and the addictive agent), irresponsibility, and feelings of self-importance often emerge progressively in the behavior of the one ad- dicted. But since these changes are hidden from ad- dicts by repression, people close to them are often confused by the changes and touchiness they en- counter in addicts and their seemingly stubborn re- fusal to see what they are obviously doing.

The addictive process is often very difficult to spot, because at first the addict can hide the addiction from others (and even from him- or herself) by only spo- radically or periodically behaving addictively. For ex- ample, an alcoholic may go on a bender only once in a while and not drink at all in between.

But at the same time the alcoholic or addict may have several different manifestations of the under- lying addictive disease. When an alcoholic is not drink- ing, for instance, he or she may be compulsively working or eating. Thus one addictive behavior may mask another. A person working addictively does not seem to be doing anything like the same thing a person drinking heavily or bingeing on food is doing. Yet all three may be manifestations of the same underlying addictive disease.

The Progressive Nature of the Disease

It is almost universally true that all addictive behaviors are progressive, leading toward dysfunction and death. Therefore, addicts may finally be led to an awareness of the addictive nature of their behavior by the progressive increase of pain from the mistakes made and their consequences, from physical and emotional symptoms, or from the growing loneliness, or disrupted life-style. The character defects and tendency toward isolation become apparent, and the addict realizes that he or she is powerless alone to stop the addictive behavior, which is "no longer worth it." At that point help may be at hand.

Causes of Addiction

Milkman and Shaffer point out that there is little agreement about the basic causes of addictive disorders.[3] Pharmacologists suggest pharmacologic problems; psychologists and psychiatrists often read into the data about addictions problems of learning, compulsion, or ego function. Physiologists tend to focus on problems related to withdrawal, metabolism, or organs affected by chemical agents. And sociologists, politicians, lawyers, and police look at the causes of addiction in terms of social regulation, peer pressure, environmental focus, legal control, criminals, and deterrents. But at present, "no single theory dominates thinking in the field of addictive behavior."[4]

As one reads the literature concerning the possible causes of addictions, it becomes apparent that each scientific discipline that has focused attention on addictions is still wrestling with many variables from that discipline's own perspective. And instead of dealing with *root* causes, science is still at the stage of filtering the behavioral data through its own grids to begin to "build structures for further study." As L. J. Hatterer points out, the problem of "causes" is very complex. There are shifting causes at different phases of a person's life that "breed addictiveness."[5]

The Disease Masks Its Cause

Once the addictive process starts and becomes a full-blown addiction in a person's life, those casual factors are no longer visible. The strong compulsion takes over, becoming "autonomous and self-perpetuating." And the initial cause or causes "often remain unrevealed and unrelated to the perpetuation of the process, which has developed a life of its own."[6]

The Religious Attitude Toward Addictions

Traditionally, when religious spokespersons have focused on addictions, their remarks have been one form or another of moral judgment and censure for the "weak will" and "lack of resolve" of the addicted person, who broke promises and abused people by not being able to stop the addictive behavior. The immoral and antisocial behavior of the addict while acting out an addiction was condemned. In more recent years many religious leaders have come to realize that addiction is a compulsive *disease* and that the addict cannot conquer the disease and "straighten up" by the use of willpower alone. This recognition has led to a less judgmental and more understanding view of addictions. But in any case, most traditional religious literature has dealt with addictions only with reference to chemical agents.

Evidence of the Underlying Disease

Several years ago, however, in chemical dependency treatment centers a new understanding began to emerge. The families of different sorts of addicts began to show up and ask for treatment. The family members were plagued with overwhelming feelings of fear, anger, pain, shame, and guilt. And they seemed to be bound to the alcoholic in a sick and addictive way, just as the alcoholic was bound to a chemical agent. They excused the alcoholic's behavior and seemed to have a persistent delusion that if they were just good enough and helped enough the alcoholic would quit drinking. And then they would get over their bad feelings about *themselves*.

At first the cause of the family members' distress was thought to be the stress of living with a seriously addicted person. But when the addict got into recovery and was no longer using chemicals, the family members' distress and symptoms often continued—even escalated. It was then that therapists began to realize that there was a separate addictive disease operating in the family members. It was as if they used the addict as an "addictive substance" to blot out and attempt to cover the same feelings of worthlessness that the alcoholic used alcohol to deal with. As the addict husband, for instance, was trying to blot out or cope with his threatening feelings with alcohol, the family members were trying to deal with the very same feelings by an addiction to the alcoholic and the cure of the dysfunctional behavior. This addiction to people came to be called codependence or codependency.

Pia Mellody points out that if one removes alcohol or drugs from the life of an alcoholic or drug addict, there will be left the same basic underlying emotional disease that is found in the codependent, with its intense self-centeredness, need to control people, and insatiable craving for approval and love.[7]

And although Mellody believes that codependence has roots in the childhood abuse experienced by the patient, this disease also seems to stem from that which I have described as Sin (in the life of the parent of the codependent).

How Are Sin and Addiction Related?

In chapter 3 I described Sin in terms of the universal dilemma of self-centeredness that has plagued men and women from the beginning. Sin stems from a deep conflict in human nature and experience, the something "broken" that cannot be "fixed" or corrected by all the success, effort, money, sex, power, or ability in the world. I said that his brokenness or separation is experienced as a haunting and fearful sense of being separated and unworthy and expresses itself in feelings of fear, anger, shame, guilt, or pain. We search the world over for someone or something we can control that will take away these painful feelings of inadequacy and we will become strongly attached or even addicted to any person, substance, behavior, or goal that promises to relieve or blot out our pain and sense of alienation.

As our fear that we will not get what we want grows, our striving increases until we are addicted to our self-centered thoughts, wants, and lusts for more than our share of life.

Sin: The Source of the Underlying Dynamic

It is the thesis of this book that this blinding self-absorption called Sin—however well it may be disguised by our civilized exteriors—is the same elusive underlying dynamic as that in the life of the traditional chemical addict. Sin is the driving dynamic that leads addicts to fasten upon an addictive chemical or behavior that promises to fulfill their self-centered and often grandiose dreams and to blot out the feelings that threaten to overwhelm them. Sin is the universal addiction to self that develops when individuals put themselves in the center of their personal world in a way that leads to abuse of others and self. Sin causes sinners to seek instant gratification, to be first, and to get more than their share—now. Chemical addicts are persons trapped by Sin who fasten onto a destructive mind-altering chemical to which they are especially physically sensitive (in an allergic sense). The effect of the chemical accelerates the underlying self-centered disease process and makes it more visible and identifiable. But the same underlying Sin-disease is in us all (Rom. 3:23).

Specific Similarities Between Sin and Addiction

Self-centered sinners, like chemical addicts, look for a mental or physical high or good feeling to cover up their painful feelings. They want to be "number one," to get what it takes to feel OK, successful, regardless of the cost to others. Sin, like chemical addiction, is compulsive and repeats itself in the face of the high risk of destruction of important relationships and material and social prosperity.

Sin, like chemical addiction, is progressive and demands "more and more" to get the same good feelings. Yet sinners, like chemical addicts, can't stop their self-defeating, self-centered behavior even when it is apparent to others that it may destroy relationships and even themselves.

Sin, like traditional addiction, leads to an increase of tension, anxiety, depression, guilt, shame, suspicion, and fear and to mood swings, physical and emotional deterioration of life-style, and destructive confrontations in one's intimate relationships.

Sin, like traditional addiction, leads to an exaggeration of character defects such as dishonesty, manipulation of people, blaming, gossiping, insatiability (with respect to attention, power, money, etc.), irresponsibility (often hidden behind respectable busyness), and an exaggerated sense of the importance of his or her life and/or work (often cloaked in an appearance of humility).

Sin, like traditional addiction, is sometimes hard to spot because sinners, like addicts, are clever at hiding and switching behaviors that might reveal the extent of their self-centeredness.

Like chemical addicts, persons suffering from the Sin-disease can hide their selfish behavior behind a mask of benevolence or even religion. Or if about to be caught at their Sin, they can switch to a new way of playing God and avoid being detected. For example, a powerful and controlling mother may become bedridden. From that bed she can manipulate and control an entire family and get exactly what she wants without having to exercise any of the outward power she has lost through her sickness—she can do this by simply threatening subtly to die or to get sicker. But the self-centered and controlling behavior to get the attention and compliance she wants is no less real because of her weak, benevolent appearance or her change in tactics.

Given enough time, however, the progressive nature of the Sin-disease, like chemical addiction, will destroy the sinner's judgment, and bring him or her down. History is replete with examples of men and women who became so grandiose that they mistook their self-centered delusions of godliness and infallibility for the real thing. Such people on the big stage of history, like Adolph Hitler, for example, made decisions that destroyed them before they could even become aware of the operation of the Sin-disease in their lives. But in our own families or neighborhoods there are many examples of parents, husbands, wives, or teenagers whose blind and destructive self-centeredness is evident to everyone but them.

As I shall attempt to demonstrate in the following chapters (and to the person trapped by the disease, this is the most startling thing about Sin), "denial" is the chief characteristic of Sin, as it is of traditional addiction: neither addicts nor sinners can see the extent to which their addiction is ruining their own lives or relationships. This makes both chronic addicts and self-absorbed sinners hard to treat—both are honestly unaware of the disease's effect on them.

Sinners, like traditional addicts, will usually not go for help until the progressive nature of the disease leads to such isolation, fear, and loneliness that it is apparent to them that their self-centered behaviors will not bring relief anymore, and that they are powerless to fix things up alone. For example, the philandering husband wakes up to find his wife and children have left him and will not come back. His sexual escapades seem hollow and no longer bring satisfaction.

Beneath the facade of the self-addicted sinner is a diseased and dysfunctional personal world that from the inside appears strikingly similar to that of the compulsive addict, a world filled with anxiety and a sense of being crazy at times. Both addicts and sinners vacillate between exaggerated feelings of being strong and unique and weak, helpless feelings of dependency and wanting someone else to care for them. Finally, as the disease develops, the threat of being overwhelmed by outsized feelings of fear, anger, guilt, shame, or pain is always lurking just out of sight in the lives of both addicts and self-addicted sinners—to drive them to despair...or help.

The Good News Is That There Is Recovery from the Invisible "Addiction" of Sin

The good news is that as one becomes aware that one may be caught in the grips of an addictive self-absorption, whether or not a chemical is involved, there is an effective way of getting into recovery.

Perhaps the fastest growing spiritual movement in the world today is the Twelve-Step program. The groups founded on the Twelve Steps are having phenomenal success in helping people into recovery from addictions to chemicals, food, work, sex, people, intensity, emotional turmoil, and the bad self-image that comes from having been raised in a dysfunctional family.

And to many people in the church the amazing thing about this movement is that it is based solidly on the biblical way of honestly facing one's powerlessness and self-centeredness and surrendering one's will and life to God. The "Twelve Steps" have been hammered out on the anvil of pain in the lives of hundreds of thousands of men and women who have seen their powerlessness without God to overcome (or even see) much of the underlying disease. With God's and each other's help they have come to see and control the addictive spiritual malady that was destroying their happiness and keeping them from serenity and joy in their lives and relationships.

It is my strong belief that the biblical story describes Sin in a way that indicates it is the underlying matrix or seedbed out of which all addictive and other destructive behaviors arise. And if this is true, then perhaps those of us who find our roots in a biblical heritage can use what has been learned about addictive behavior and its alleviation. Perhaps, once more, through a surrender to God we can begin to see a way with God's help (and each other's) to unmask the Sin in our own lives and let God heal us of our frustration and loneliness—before the Sin-disease destroys our relationships, our happiness, and even our lives.

The rest of this book is about:

The personal nature and effects of the disease caused by Sin;

The baffling strategies Sin uses to hide its action in our lives from our own view;

A way of confronting the Sin-disease with God's help and learning to live and grow together through intentional change.

II

The Sin-Disease

6

An Introduction to the Sin-Disease

In the earliest accounts of life in Genesis, the Bible presents us with a picture of the first man and woman in a virtual paradise, owned and operated by God. God told them the limits of their authority and gave them freedom. But as soon as they were left alone they ignored the reality of their situation—who God was and who they were—and tried to be God, to get control and be number one in paradise. And in doing this they fouled up their relationships to God and his paradise, to each other, and to themselves.

The rest of the biblical narrative tells the story of the struggle of men and women to overcome the separation caused by this self-centered and self-defeating tendency toward grandiosity and control, which causes us to try getting what we want when we want it—in spite of the needs of others and the will of God. Some people see the root of Sin as our mistrust of God. He offered Adam and Eve all they needed to be happy, but they didn't trust God's offer and tried to take control of the garden and all in it as if they were God themselves. When caught they were ashamed but continued to struggle for control. This struggle includes the way we pass the buck and twist the truth to make us look righteous when we're caught Sinning.

Throughout the Bible we see God ever reaching out to help his people in their freedom to overcome their lonely separation. The battle is waged at many different levels. Men and women, institutions, and nations struggle with the destructive, selfish behaviors Sin causes. The effects of inflated selfishness have spread to the farthest corners of the earth from that initial tendency to take God's place and be number one, and this diseased behavior sooner or later leads to increased misery and lonely depression.

Is It Valid to Call Sin a Disease?

The American Medical Association says that a disease must have

a. definable onset

b. symptoms

c. a predictable outcome

Sin is apparently a spontaneous human reaction to the holy and godlike. As each human being responds to the godlike in his or her experience by trying to replace it as the God/center, Sin has its onset in that person's behavioral life. The symptoms of the disease of Sin are many: swollen self-importance, manipulation and using of people for our pleasure, all kinds of abuse, lying and denial of the truth about our selfishness, and the many symptoms surrounding and supporting our repression of the truth about our motives (e.g., compulsive and addictive behaviors such as addictions to work, intensity, sex, food, money, drugs, and alcohol). The predictable outcome of the disease is fear, isolation, paranoia, increasing compulsiveness, physical symptoms, "accidents," and death.

The Sin-disease is an affliction present in all human societies, and its symptoms come to light in men's and women's selfish (and self-destructive) behavior. The Bible is clear that the final payoff of Sin is death (Rom. 6:23). Even if the Sin-disease is not technically a disease, it certainly acts like one.

You may say, "But if we call Sin a disease does that mean that we are no longer responsible for it?" No. That's a paradox. Sin is a disease, but because we are free, we *choose* to Sin, to put ourselves in the center where only God belongs. We don't *have* to Sin, but history indicates that we all *do* Sin. As the theologian Reinhold Niebuhr put it, in effect, it is "inevitable though not necessary" that human beings Sin. And since God has offered each of us his power to defeat Sin, we are responsible for a decision not to accept his offer and use that power to enter his battle against the Disease.

How Does the Disease Establish a Foothold in Our Lives?

How does this Sin-disease get into each of our lives? And why don't we give it up.[1] The Bible indicates that it got into human beings in the beginning, through Adam and Eve.[2]

There is a progressive process in each of our lives that we don't talk about much. As children we try and fail at certain things, simply because we are young and don't have the ability to do everything. Because grown-ups appear to us as able to do anything they try to do, and because they seem to expect us to have only appropriate thoughts and feelings, we feel inadequate and unloved when we have thoughts or feelings or behave in ways that are not accepted by the ones who care for us.

Since all parents are gripped by Sin, they teach us to expect to get what we want from people (since they appear to—at least from us), in the same way as they expect us to always "do it right" and please them. We want to be wise and right as they seem to be or think they are, and we certainly want them to love us. When we can't perform perfectly, we are afraid we may be rejected and/or punished, so we lie and blame things on brothers or sisters or others—as Adam and Eve did. We must defend our behavior, because we feel we'll be worthless and rejected if we are "wrong." But outright lying makes us feel bad about ourselves, since we are also supposed to be honest. We feel guilty. So we have a real dilemma: How do we cover up our sins and mistakes—which we all commit—without lying?

The Battle with Conscience: An Agonizing Struggle

A part of us seeks and clings to what we consider to be right. Our "conscience" polices our decisions according to our ideas of honesty and rightness. When we go against those values, whatever they are, we feel guilt or shame and judge ourselves to be unacceptable. For example, when we are under pressure and lie about why we were late to a meeting or when we gloss over a nondeductible item and leave it on our tax return or expense account, we feel a vague (or sharp) sense of uneasiness—and we quickly try to move on to other thoughts. Often Sins seems to attack us at the point of conflict between some value and a desire to gratify a self-centered greed or lust that contradicts that value. We want to be moral people, but we are also selfish and want to do and to have what feels good, regardless of the consequences. Sex is a prime example.

Years ago I talked to a man who had a good marriage to a lovely woman he was very fond of. But he liked to have casual affairs with younger women. When confronted with a choice, he decided to leave the marriage—even though he admitted that was stupid. He began to eat compulsively and withdrew into himself, alienating many of his former friends. He is now a sad, lonely man who is obviously destroying himself—even though he has everything he could want materially—but he still won't give up his casual sexual affairs.

If we were totally rational people, "right value"

would always win out in such conflicts, since that's what we *say* we want. But we are in the center where God should be. And when we *really* want something that goes against our value code, we can amass a great deal of energy to go for it, even if the goal is "wrong" in our eyes. And sometimes we want the "unrighteous" goal so much that we go ahead and transgress our values, telling ourselves that we will handle the guilt and possible punishment later. As children we steal the party candy from the kitchen and risk the spanking. As adults we misrepresent the facts in a business deal to make a lot of money.

But those of us who can't stand the pain of our guilt get into a more complicated scenario. Our need to "do it right" may be *enormous*. Let's say a little girl is so threatened by guilt feelings that she does not steal the candy. Since she wants so much to be righteous yet wants the candy a lot too, the conflict she feels is greatly increased. How can she get what she wants that contradicts her values and still be righteous?

Denial: An (Almost) Perfect Out—Now You See It, Now You Don't!

Our Sin offers us a seemingly perfect way out of this painful dilemma. Through a process called denial we can rationalize and trick ourselves into thinking we aren't exactly transgressing our values, or that, if we are, it is actually for the good of the person we are hurting. For example, the husband I spoke of earlier said that being unfaithful to his spouse took the pressure off her to perform sexually. He had to deny to himself a *lot* of things he knew about her feelings and values to come up with that bizarre logic so he could get what he wanted.

But if denial in the form of rationalization doesn't work for him, he can unconsciously repress or forget the fact that there is a dilemma at all![3] He can go ahead and do the thing that for him is "not right" and simply submerge the "value" he is transgressing into his unconscious mind so that he doesn't even see it. He denies that he places value on marital fidelity while he is being unfaithful. Later he can "stop his ears" (deny the cry of his conscience) with regard to this act. He can say to himself and to God in his prayers that he is still righteous, because while he is praying he is not *conscious* of having transgressed any value— except possibly in some vague, distant, or unrelated way.

This scenario may seem bizarre at first, but I have never known anyone who didn't do this sort of lying to him- or herself to excuse behavior that gratified some self-centered desire—small or large—at the expense of integrity or relationships, or both. The "crime" might be gossiping about a friend under the guise of "concern." We Christians are often terrible about this. Or we may play golf or bridge constantly or stay occupied at all kinds of busy-ness that shuts out our family but *say* (and believe) that we spend a great deal of quality time with them. And only the family members know that they do not have our real attention.

The true crime is self-centeredness, emotional desertion and abuse of others, about which we are in denial. From the outside our delusion may look true—even to us.

We do not "know" when we are doing this. The best, even the most religious, people in the world would not be aware of engaging in this sort of denial unless someone was honest enough to tell them. Even then, the tendency is to be defensive and not to believe the honest party; remember, the discrepancies between our behavior and our view of ourselves are *not* conscious to us. Our rationalizations may seem bizarre to others, but we defend ourselves, have all kinds of "reasons" for our self-centered behavior, and claim we're right.

I knew a man who used to leave his wife and two babies alone on weekends while he played golf and drank beer with his boss or prospective clients. The couple had no help and couldn't afford money for babysitters, so the wife was alone with her babies seven days a week. The man felt he was being a good husband and father and taking care of his family—even though his wife told him repeatedly in tears how desperately she needed him on weekends. The man is very intelligent, and his blindness to what was really happening with his family was almost unbelievable. He was "in denial."

Some Bad Side Effects of Denial

In order to help us avoid unpleasant truths about our behavior without "lying," our Sin-disease provides a way for us to hide from ourselves the sins and the real but unacceptable thoughts, feelings, and failures we all have. At an early age we start the process of unconsciously stuffing our sins and "failures to be perfect" out of sight in the basements of our lives and eventually out of sight from ourselves. But these denied behaviors have feelings attached to them (e.g., guilt, shame, fear, pain, and anger).

And the problem is that these repressed feelings have *energy* in them. And this energy causes us to do some "irrational" things.

Sometimes when we can't face our feelings and we stuff them out of our sight, we project them onto others. For instance, when we feel stupid or cowardly or hate someone and can't face these feelings, we may call our mate (or one of our children or someone of another race, or criminals, or our enemies) stupid or cowardly and say *they* hate *us*. We dump our denied Sin and feelings onto others, and they feel them when we won't. This is called projection. And when family members (or a whole group of people) buy into the negative feelings projected at them (which may not be true at all), they can feel like the scum of the earth, too bad to ever be forgiven. And they don't know why. When this happens the one denying feelings and the ones accepting the projected feelings are equally caught by the Sin-disease. This is an example of the ripple effect hiding our unacceptable reality from ourselves through denial can have.[4]

In denial, we are unconsciously trying to lock away our monstrous selves, which we fear might get us rejected by people we need, or by God. Many of us, in our insecurity about our denied reality, go to great lengths to look and sound "adequate" or even righteous. We have "denied" to ourselves those things that would contradict that image. This often leads to an exaggerated need to be "right" and a strong reluctance to admit being wrong. Without ever realizing it (and to varying degrees), many of us have created a delusion in which to live, a delusion to make us feel OK about who we are: we defend that delusion at the cost of family, friends, jobs, and even health.

In my case I felt that God had given me a gift of speaking and writing and that I should use it. I saw myself as an unselfish man sharing my time and abilities lavishly with God's people. But I denied to myself that I was busy becoming "well known" in the part of the religious world in which I traveled—I would have been very angry had anyone accused me of this, for it did not fit my delusion of humility.

This is one example of how the Sin uses denial to distort the truth so that we can no longer be who God made us to be. We must hide from each other as Adam and Eve hid from God, and it is in this hiding of reality and recreating ourselves in a false image that we are imprisoned by the Sin-disease.

All Have Sinned

From an early age, it seems, we unconsciously and consciously reshape the truth about ourselves, hoping to become acceptable to others and to us. My experience has been that we seal off—along with the unacceptable feelings—the positive qualities and dreams we might fulfill but don't try. We don't try our dreams since we fear we might fail and reveal our human weaknesses. Or we won't try because we feel we don't deserve to be happy and succeed because of our "worthless, sinful" inner feelings.

A Distorted Picture

By the time we reach adulthood, many of us have a distorted picture of ourselves. This distortion of our reality can confuse our families and will tend to direct our children along the same path of denial and delusion we're on. The sins of the parents are indeed visited upon their children to the third and fourth generations (Exod. 20:5).

In a sense it is almost certain that we will become self-deceivers and then liars (to defend our delusion) and be unaware of it. Some people may be offended at the notion that they are liars; I certainly would have been a few years ago. But the clinical and biblical evidence points to the fact that all people Sin this way to some degree—even though they are not aware of it or may call it "exaggeration" or use some other less incriminating name. (See 1 John 1:8, etc.)[5]

And so we become a people in hiding, living in the bondage of denied or undealt-with sins and failures of the past that erode our confidence in our good qualities, our true abilities, and our self-worth.

Of course all Sinful behaviors and lies are not denied. We are conscious of many of our sins of omission and commission and are conscious of the guilt and shame they cause us when we can't control them. And we sometimes feel trapped by *these* uncomfortable feelings.

But those unacceptable thoughts and behaviors we

have denied truly baffle us: we feel anxious and sometimes unworthy but can't see what we've done wrong,
even when people tell us we are hurting them with
certain "thought-less" behaviors. We are unaware that
we are imprisoned. We may appear to ourselves and
even to others as successful, respectable, upright, and
aware people. The Pharisees are pictured in the New
Testament as people who saw themselves as respectable and righteous. And yet Jesus pointed repeatedly
to their repressed sins and the danger of not facing
themselves (Luke 11:39,40).

But how does denial look from the *inside*—since by
definition we are not aware of our own denied reality?

7

Denial: Some X-Ray Pictures

In this chapter I will give some pictures, from different angles, of the way denial works in people's lives. Since we can only see it operating in the lives of others, and we resist (almost to the death sometimes) seeing our own denial, it is often difficult to describe this disease process adequately from an objective viewpoint. So I will try to give a personal report of my own painful discovery of the operation of denial in my life along with examples of some of the other "weapons" the Sin-disease uses to distort reality and keep us from discovering the harmful and self-destructive nature of our self-centered behavior.

A Personal Report

For years I had seen this denial process happen to other men and women who came to me for counsel.

Sometimes it was hard to understand why they couldn't see that they were being arrogant, overbearing, terribly insensitive, and even abusive to members of their families or to their employees. Yet I knew these men and women well enough to realize that they honestly could not see the destructive nature and effects of their behavior.

But when I went for help I finally saw the Sin-disease in myself. That was when I began to understand why I didn't comprehend the self-centered and controlling nature of my "well-meaning" behavior to people around me.

This is a brief picture of what happened to me, an independent business consultant and a religious writer and speaker.

In my mind's eye I was a business consultant who also spent a lot of time helping others to find God and to live honestly in their relationships to him and others as I tried to do these things.

My first clue to the fact that all was not as it seemed was that, although I was a calm, understanding counselor, I was very touchy and defensive at any hint of criticism at home.

Eventually, in my rush to get everything done, I quit "having the time" to listen patiently to people as individuals. I became impatient with people who wouldn't "face their problems," though I did not let this show. I also got impatient with "the church" and subtly switched from witnessing to "preaching at" the institution, trying to change it into my image of what it should be. These compulsive behaviors occupied more and more of my time. Although I still *felt* like a loving, helpful Christian, unconsciously I was *be-*

having like an ungrateful and compulsive "religious star" of some kind. But at the time these things were happening I was not aware of them. I was "in denial."

With help I came to see that I had a tendency to manipulate people in my need to be "famous," but my denial had kept me unaware of this. I had also stuffed away the feelings of anger and resentment I had that didn't fit my image of myself as a loving Christian. (Consciously I just thought I'd been blessed with a good disposition, but I discovered that deep inside I had a *lot* of denied feelings.)

I was helped to see that beneath that touchy defensiveness I felt whenever anyone in my family criticized me was a bottomless cistern of denied resentment and pain and the fear of being discovered as "not good enough."

Compulsive Behavior—the Disease's "Game" to Hide Reality

I learned that obsessive thoughts and compulsive behaviors can constitute a sort of glittering inner wall that the Sin-disease uses to hide from us the selfish and grandiose nature of our behavior and our negative feelings about it. These compulsions and obsessions can become a kind of "hand-held shield" or shifting "fake-out" game. They can distract us from having to face unacceptable (denied) current behaviors or unacceptable memories from the past that may be trying to surface in our consciousness and reveal us to ourselves. So by engaging in certain compulsive behaviors (working compulsively, eating too much, drinking too much, taking tranquilizers, engaging in compulsive sexual thoughts and behaviors, being addicted to people-pleasing or even church work) we can "fill our lives" and avoid facing our feelings, our sins, and our deepest reality—that God could use in our lives to help us see ourselves and grow spiritually.

For example, I know a man whose marriage was in trouble. He and his wife were barely communicating, even about superficial things. But this man would not face the seriousness of his marital problems. Instead he began working compulsively, night and day. Within a few years, by working and traveling constantly, he had developed a successful company and national recognition in his field. In the meantime he had bought his wife expensive gifts and said his marriage was much better. But in counseling he finally became aware that he had deserted his wife emotionally in the name of business and not faced their relationship—which by now was almost beyond repair.

As our compulsions increase, we lose any spontaneous sense of joy. We begin feeling more and more anxious, and we stifle our relationships through our increasing self-centered focus on our agenda. At last we may be crying out for some peace, some relief from the prison of our compulsive working—or other compulsions or addictions—and are amazed at the extent to which we have lost touch with family and friends.

The tragedy is that we cannot receive help and a new start until we know we need it. Even Jesus said that those who know they are sick and need a physician are those to whom he came (Luke 5:31, 32). And yet, by its nature, denial keeps us from recognizing and admitting that we can't handle things alone.

From the Inside Denial Is Very Confusing

Part of the Disease's strategy is (in line with its urging us to keep ourselves in the controlling center where only God belongs) to tell us in a dozen ways that "we can do it by *ourselves*." I was told as a little boy, "Don't bother Daddy, he's tired." I was supposed "to do it myself" and not to bother other people with my needs. And although my mother meant well, this sort of thinking only made me more lonely and centered in myself.

When as an adult I became a work addict, I worked night and day to try to meet all the needs of everyone in my life. As I said earlier, people would call at all hours of the night, and I would counsel them. I prayed for dozens of people by name daily. I worked weekends and traveled constantly. I'd make frantic efforts at meeting my family's needs when I came home.

Consciously I saw all this working away from home as part of my ministry for God. I was confused when my family didn't always cheer and think what I was doing was great. But with help I finally saw that all my "unselfish giving of myself," which strangers applauded, only made me—like my father—too tired and busy to relate to my family in a healthy way.

I realized later that it was quite presumptuous of me to try to meet all those strangers' needs. Who in the world did I think I was? And by my compulsive working I was avoiding facing my insensitivity and anger, and my fears and inadequacies as a father and husband. Secretly I was also miserable and very confused. It didn't seem fair.

Was I the only person not allowed to have rest and recreation? Was I a man who was excused from the normal illnesses and pressures of life and could work twelve, fifteen, eighteen hours a day without its affecting my health? I apparently thought that I was called to do more than other people. I was special. I thought I was unique—which, in fact, turned out to be almost "terminally" unique. This was Sin-inspired behavior, but in my denial I saw it only as "commitment." The tricky thing is that part of it was, but what I was calling dedication was in part a symptom of the Sin-disease that manifested itself in my addiction to work.

Finally I was helped to see that my compulsive working had become a wall of denial behind which sat a lonely, insecure person who was trying to manipulate people and circumstances to hide his self-centered need to be number one. Later it was a great blow to my ego to discover that I had used the fact that my work was "for God" as a way to deny a great deal of the personal reality in my life.

The Cunning Nature of the Sin-Disease

I couldn't believe how subtle and cunning the Disease is and how, without being aware I was doing it, I continually tried to get back in control and look good in all situations. The surprising thing is that it doesn't seem to matter if one is very intelligent or very dumb; the Disease cons us into really believing that what we are doing or want to do is all right—even if the objective truth (which the people around us, even children sometimes, can see clearly) is that the course we want to take may be disastrous for us.

The "Respectable" Tools of Denial

Sometimes people—especially religious people—do not realize that when they use things like food, work, cigarettes, or tranquilizers to "quiet their nerves" they are keeping themselves from facing the anxieties and denial in their lives as much as if they were drowning them in alcohol. Many fine Christians, for instance, eat a piece of cake and drink a glass of milk when they feel rejected—until they have gained enough weight to be in physical danger. And yet often they will not face the fact that they have a problem with food—though everyone around them can see the obvious effects of the Sin-disease and its denial.

People who are overweight are told routinely that they are endangering their hearts or other vital organs and bones, yet they continue to overeat and/or stuff their families. Not long ago I talked to a very obese single man who lives alone. He has been told by his doctor that if he does not lose a great deal of weight his joints, which are deteriorating, are going to become useless, and he will not be able to walk. And yet this man was eating a huge dinner and two desserts as we talked. I felt sad as I saw the extent of his denial.[1]

The excessive use of tranquilizers and sleeping pills,

excessive smoking, drinking, working, religious work, and addictions to excitement, to sex, and to people (including our own children)—all these things are crippling "normal people" daily. The startling fact is that, because of denial, we only see the destructive nature of these things clearly in the lives of *other* people. We minimize our own compulsive and addictive behaviors and *honestly believe* that we don't have a problem.

Symptoms of Denial: Anxiety, Shame, Guilt, and "Surprising Reactions"

Eventually, continuing to deny certain painful areas of reality in life and unconsciously burying certain feelings, one begins to behave in more and more baffling or embarrassing ways. One may feel shame or guilt over almost anything. For instance, having made the simple social blunder of calling someone by the wrong name, I have often felt a wave of shame and embarrassment—when in fact such mistakes happen to most people.

When I feel guilty about something, I often react by being very angry at someone else. I get angry to "change the subject" and get the monkey off my back, because I hate to be wrong. Or I beat myself for "what a fool I've been." When I start a diet and break it, I feel shame. Why? Who cares if I break my diet (besides me)? Most people don't even know about it. I have often felt excessive guilt or been filled with shame simply at not behaving perfectly, because I hadn't dealt with the reservoir of denied sins, guilt, and failure filling the basement of my life. I lived in fear of somehow being "revealed" as inadequate, not realizing that this related to the mass of denied material in my unconscious. When the reaction is far greater than the behavior would normally call for, it is almost certain that part of the "cause" is unconscious and has perhaps been denied.[2]

Sometimes the sadness, anger, or other denied feelings just come popping out into one's consciousness at the most unexpected times in reaction to some "ordinary" event (e.g., unexpected tears at seeing a laughing child playing or hearing a song on the radio, or a burst of anger or resentment at some innocuous remark).

I have often unconsciously hidden my feelings of pain or hurt pride with anger. A family member can say "good morning" the wrong way and catch a load of leaking repressed anger, to my surprise and dismay. Or I may catch myself saying something sarcastic to an old friend when I didn't have any *conscious* intention of doing so. And sometimes when I am denying my feelings, I operate in a kind of perceptual fog; I can't remember things like where I put something or what I came to the grocery store to get.[3]

We are, in effect, in bondage to the feelings that we will not face, and to the cunning Disease that helped us bury them.

The "Destination" of Sin Is Eventually Death

The danger of our not taking this Sin-disease seriously is that it leads us subtly and progressively to-

ward isolation and death—spiritual or physical.
People who continue to ignore and repress the physical and emotional symptoms through which their denied feelings and sins are crying out to be heard often
try to bury them deeper through increased compulsive behavior and wind up with serious, even terminal,
physical or emotional illness. Of course, I am not
blaming *all* physical symptoms and emotional illness
on sin and denial. As Scott Peck has pointed out, all
physical symptoms have four component-causes,
which vary in importance (psychological, spiritual, sociological, and somatic). But I am saying that the Disease can contribute significantly to the causes in all
four areas.

An example of the insanity to which the Sin-disease
(through denial) can take us was a friend of ours
whom I'll call Eldon. Eldon was in his early fifties. He
was vice-president of an international corporation and
had offices in both New York and California. His
career was skyrocketing. He was apparently in good
physical condition, but he smoked several packs of
cigarettes a day. Eldon was told by his boss that he
should get a physical examination every year. In fact,
his company gave him a free annual physical at the
Mayo Clinic. But Eldon refused to go, even though
taking the physical was "compulsory." His personal
doctor had told him repeatedly that he was smoking
too much and that it was getting pretty serious. Although he was a brilliant executive, Eldon kept ignoring his symptoms, saying his smoking was "no
problem," and he kept refusing to get the physical.

Suddenly one day he had a great deal of trouble
breathing, went to the hospital, and found out he had

cancer of the lung due to his smoking; he died within a short time.

Another irrational and deadly way the Disease uses denial is through the amazing illusion that one is somehow indestructible, not bound by the normal rules of probability related to illness and death. This was brought home to me in a tragic way through the experience of another friend. This man, whom I'll call Harry, was president of an effective helping ministry to people in cities. He was a hard-driving, compulsive person and had built this enterprise into an outstanding organization that was helpful to hundreds of people. Harry ignored his physical health and at age forty-five had a massive coronary that almost killed him. His doctor told him that if he followed orders strictly and went very slowly there was a chance he could recover and lead a reasonably normal life but that his heart had been badly damaged and was in critical condition.

One of the things the doctor told him not to do was have sexual intercourse with his wife for a while, until the doctor gave him permission. One day shortly after he got home from the hospital Harry was in a romantic mood and called his wife into the bedroom. He began to kiss her, and it was apparent to her that he was approaching her sexually. She objected and reminded him the doctor had warned that it could kill him. His comment was, "What a way to go." He talked her into making love to him, had an orgasm, and died from the coronary that followed.

These were two outstanding and brilliant men who wanted to live and who had a great deal to offer other people. They both disregarded the advice of experts whom they respected. They somehow hid the reality of their lives from themselves, and as a result both died. This sort of behavior seems very diseased and irrational. Yet physicians see people die every day for similar reasons. The Sin-disease, with its weapons of denial and delusion, is a serious and often terminal illness.

Work addicts or overeaters may never realize that their compulsive behavior is a message from God trying to warn them that there's something out of kilter at the center of their inner lives—that they have transgressed the basic rule of human life by putting themselves and their God-playing at the center where only God can make life work. The message gets louder and louder through increasingly serious emotional and then physical symptoms: emotional symptoms like anxiety, lack of sleep, depression, irrational outbursts, and resentment, and physical symptoms like headaches, arthritis, ulcers, colitis, certain heart conditions, strokes, in some cases a series of dangerous "accidents," and—some physicians believe—even cancer.

Dr. Paul Tournier in his "medicine of the whole person" made a career of telling doctors that sickness often comes from the transgression of basic values and the repressing of reality. If people don't heed the warnings of their feelings and bodies, they may be drawn toward and enmeshed in the center of an ever-tightening web of compulsion and denial. Through these defenses they continue to bury, cover, or medicate the threatening feelings of worthlessness and fear that get connected to their denied Sin and failures—and for which they see no remedy.

God keeps calling us back to face our denied reality with the silent symptom-messages of illness, which, if we "hear" them—and recognize our powerlessness to handle them alone—can make us free (see John 8:32).

Our Denial Affects Other People

Since we don't acknowledge certain feelings of anger and resentment, for instance, we sometimes (as I suggested earlier) project them onto other people and claim they are angry at us (something that is much more acceptable for a "good person" than being angry at others). But this irrational behavior makes people around us very uneasy. It's scary for them to realize that we are angry and won't acknowledge it. This can lead to divorce and other serious breaches with people we care for.[4] The bottom line is that this Sin, with its denial and delusion, constitutes a serious personal and relational illness.

So far I have said that the Sin-disease consists of the combination of several things that stem from our Sin: the selfish and abusive behaviors (sins) that result from our swollen selfishness, combined with the dynamic attempts of the Disease to hide its activities from anyone's view, including our own. This hiding is accomplished primarily through three defensive strategies: denial, delusion, and compulsive and addictive behaviors that absorb our attention so much that our own feelings, which might lead us to face our Sin, are blocked out.

Everywhere one looks the Disease is like a tornado with its denial, projection, and paranoia whirling angrily through the relationships and institutions in which we live. In the face of this gathering storm our egos swell out of all proportion, and we think we have the right to break the laws and rules that bind mere mortals and interfere in the lives of other people and groups as if we were God. We become compulsive and unreal and engage in self-limiting and addictive behaviors that threaten to destroy us as individuals and the people around us. No one—from the "highest" to the "lowest" in the land—is free from the power of Sin and its symptoms of grandiosity, denial, and delusion.

On the other hand, the confusion, the anxiety, and the fear we experience because of our denial combine to give us the sense that we are helpless to do anything about our addictions or circumstances. And as the pressure from the denied feelings increases, we may strike out at someone in our desperation or get divorced—or we may end our own lives by suicide, through drinking or with a gun. Sin is truly a sickness unto death (Rom. 6:23).

The Need for Forgiveness and a New Start

At the deepest level, we experience this profound self-centered and lonely sense of dis-ease as a conscious or semiconscious need to be loved and forgiven by somebody in authority—such as our parents. We tend to long for someone who might be able to hear what (and who) is inside us—the part of ourselves we have judged unacceptable—so we could risk seeing the whole truth and telling them. We long for someone to *know* us who will accept us with all our feelings of unworthiness.

We seem to be yearning for someone to make our relationships right, to give us a fresh start as adults, even though we may be old in terms of years. We seem to be longing for a new spiritual birth.

"But wait a minute," some people have said to me at this point. "Are you saying that we *Christians* and other religious people have denied many of our sins and have often repressed *our* most painful feelings and can't see them ourselves? I thought you said that God overcame our Sin when we responded to him. And if denial is such a big thing, where does it show up in the Bible? How does this Sin-disease and its delusion work among religious people?"

8

The Sin-Disease Among Religious People

As I've already suggested, for many, Sin is that condition of self-centered separation between a person and God that leads to alienation from other people. Finally, the taking of God's place as "the center" leads to an inner division between a person and his or her real but denied self.

But the question Christians ask is, If God won a "victory over Sin" two thousand years ago, then why is it that his people *still* have to wrestle with it in their lives today? And if the denial I speak of is such an important aspect of Sin, where *does* it show up in the Bible and in our experience in the church?

Denial and Delusion in the Bible

Throughout the Bible story there is evidence of the irrational effects of denial and delusion among God's people. When the message of God was too demanding or threatening or people wanted to replace God's will with their own, they would often either "not hear" God's message or "forget" it.

The biblical record is filled with the mystery of this particular kind of spiritual deafness, blindness, or loss of memory. Moses was thrilled to see all the people promise to obey God forever. But then when he went up on the mountain for a few days, the people "forgot" and broke their covenant—at the risk of death—as if the covenant had never existed. As a result God was ready to kill them, and only Moses' intercession saved the people from being "blotted out" (Exod. 32).

Isaiah spoke of the people's hearing but not understanding, and seeing but not perceiving. He intimated that if they could somehow see and hear the truth, and understand with their hearts, they would be healed. (See Isa. 6:9 f. and 42:18–20.) It was as if someone had built an evil wall between the people's eyes and ears and their hearts. They had spells of being spiritually blind and deaf and didn't know it.

The story of David's adultery with Bathsheba and his subsequent murder of Bathsheba's husband, Uriah, appears to be an example of the way Sin and denial work on a man of God when he is in the grip of his self-centered Sin-disease. (See 2 Sam. 11:1–12:25.) It is clear that David knew what a great wrong it was to commit adultery with Bathsheba, get her pregnant, and murder her husband to cover his sin. But in his self-centered lust David wanted Bathsheba and repressed the moral gravity of what he was doing as he committed murder to hide his sin and get her into his household. His strong feelings about such an unjust act became apparent when David was confronted by the prophet Nathan through the parable of the man who had only one small lamb. David was incensed at the wealthy man who had stolen the only lamb owned by the poor man in the parable. David shouted that the rich man in the story deserved to die! When Nathan said "*You* are the man," David's denial was immediately shattered and he saw clearly what he had done and how wrong it was.

Nathan was a spiritual genius. Although direct confrontation is seldom effective in breaking through denial, the denied life-changing truth can often get through clothed in a parable. The sudden awareness of a sinful behavior that David experienced is characteristic of the experience of coming out of denial.

In the New Testament Jesus indicated that he was teaching in parables, hoping to get around this "wall" (of denial) so that people could see and hear the truth in their hearts and be healed (Matt. 13:13). To his own disciples he said, in obvious irritation, "Having eyes do you not see, and having ears do you not hear? And do you not remember?" (Mark 8:18).

Paul's own statement of this confusing problem of denial's relation to sin after years of following Christ is amazingly perceptive and poignant—and strangely familiar:

I do not understand my own actions. For I do not do what I want, but I do the very thing I hate . . . So then it is no longer I that do it, but sin which dwells within me . . . I can will what is right, but I cannot do it. For I do not do the good I want, but the evil I do not want is what I do. Now if I do what I do not want, it is no longer I that do it, but sin which dwells within me. (Rom. 7:15–20)

Traditionally some Christians have assumed that because God "overcame Sin" they no longer have to worry about it. But the New Testament record indicates that although Sin may have been overcome at its core, each of us still has to do battle with our own Sin and the disease Sin started in the world. The poisonous serpent in the grass has been mortally wounded, but it can still bite us and kill us. There are vivid accounts of the fact that the consequences of not facing sin after becoming a Christian are serious and can even include physical death.

Denial in the Church

Today we can still do this rationalization and be in denial about God's message and our lack of response to it as a congregation. For instance, many of us would *say* that we understand that it is very important to God that we love the poor, feed the hungry, and take care of them. But then in our financial meetings we "forget" the Bible's clear words and don't vote to give money from our church to the poor at all—or give an amount so small as to be merely a token. And our programs seldom include visiting prisoners. We either rationalize that we can't afford the money or time or simply repress and deny the fact that Jesus said that those who would be in eternal life with him would do these things and those who didn't do them would "go away into eternal punishment" (see Matt. 25:31–46).

Sometimes we quibble about who "the poor" are. We often accept consciously only those parts of Scripture that fit our self-centered view of reality. For years I repressed the passages in the Bible having to do with confessing our sins to another person. I just didn't let those passages register. I read them but "denied" them.

I was terrified at the thought of being seen by another person as sinful and inadequate with some of my grubby little sins, on one hand, and of not having *enough* "macho" sins, on the other. So I preached and taught about a "God of love" who actually didn't hold people very accountable for confessing sins in such a vulnerable way. That was the way I saw it consciously, but finally the disease got so bad and I was so miserable that my denial was cracked open and the awareness I am writing about came. Now I see passages everywhere that talk about God's hatred of sin and our need to live in the light.

Also our American "rugged individualism" makes it easy for the Disease to cause us to deny the mutual interdependence the Bible is filled with. The Disease's tactic is to divide and conquer to keep us under its control. This supplanting of God's Word by our word is a classic example of the grandiosity and delusion produced by Sin.

The Evidence of the Disease is Everywhere

The evidence of our denial is everywhere. Let's say we want to be *recognized* as outstanding members of our church. We have worked hard in the church for years, but since we know that we are supposed to be "humble," we say we "don't care" if we are elected to the vestry or chosen as head of a church committee or an organization. And we really think we don't care. Yet our anger at those who are chosen and our gossiping and picking at their performance tells others that we have denied our lust for power and prominence and are living a lie—even though we do not or cannot honestly see our Sin at work. Our resentment and anxiety and our lack of peace are signaling to us that the Sin-disease is at work in our life, if we could only hear or see it.

One characteristic of the denial produced by Sin is that it almost always smacks of selfishness or is an attempt to cover up selfishness. The Disease often causes us to behave in a destructive and antisocial way, though the actual sin-*behavior* is often cloaked in respectability, "helping," and even "ministry." For instance, I have sometimes helped people in order to get them to contribute or do something else for us in the church. I would call on them and welcome them warmly because we needed church school teachers or their financial pledge. This offering people love and fellowship when in fact we are using them for our own ends can be very destructive to the recipients of our attentions when they find out that they have been tricked and used in the name of love. Yet I was oblivious of my Sin in this area and was surprised that "my" new people sometimes didn't stick around.

Sin Is Always Self-Destructive Too

In the end the denied behavior inspired by Sin is always *self*-destructive too. For instance, let's say a minister honestly sets out with intense activity to build a big church for God when in fact his true—but denied and unconscious motive—is the building of a successful vocational record for himself and a monument to his own validity as a person. He may wind up lonely and disillusioned and controlled by compulsive work or other behaviors of the Sin-disease without ever knowing what happened to him.

I can now see that this was part of what occurred in my life as a professional religious speaker. And I am convinced that much of the burnout, alcoholism, and other addictions and compulsions among the clergy and laity are the result of living in denial and delusion. We lose track of the nature and focus of our commitment and our feelings of authenticity as human beings. The tragedy is that when the burnout comes we seldom know what hit us.

9

Facing Our Own Reality: Behaviors and Stuffed Feelings

The heart is deceitful above all things, and desperately corrupt; who can understand it?

JEREMIAH 17:9

It seems that as we begin unconsciously to hide things from other people, from ourselves, and from God, we have an increasing need to "recreate" reality so that we won't have to face the growing dissonance between our values and our behavior, between our acceptable and unacceptable sides.

Like the Pharisees of Jesus' time, we "respectable ones" may hide enough of our selfish motives and behavior from ourselves that we start believing we are the righteous persons we want very much to be. And when we feel guilty or unacceptable we sometimes begin to increase the number of "righteous acts" and "unselfish things" we *do*—to prove to God and to ourselves that we are, in fact, good people. This compensatory religious activity reinforces the strength of our denial.

This was evidently what happened to the Pharisees against whom Jesus made his most bitter attacks. They were going through all the outward rituals to show each other how righteous they were. And evidently they *were* faithful attenders and *did* work hard at their faith. But as Jesus said, inside, in their motivations and the hidden areas of their hearts, they were rotting like dead men's bones. The Sin-disease was winning in many of their lives, and they were oblivious to their own Sin (see Matt. 23:25–28). They were driven to more and more compulsive religious behavior to cover their anxiety and to keep from facing their denial. Unfortunately the same dynamic still works in the lives of many of us today who see ourselves as the people in the white hats.

But if this is true, why don't people get help and stop this irrational and self-defeating behavior?

Denial and Delusion in Everyday Experience

From my experience, counseling and talking to other people who have also discovered the spiritually crippling nature of this disease in their lives, it seems that the two characteristics of the Sin-disease that I have been discussing, "denial" and "delusion," are almost universal. Denial by definition means not being able to see the ever-widening split between what one says and what one is. So without some sort of shock or intervention people do not know they need to go for help. It's not that such a person doesn't *want* to see, it's that he or she *cannot*.[1]

Delusion is seeing things that are true and acting as if they are *not* true. Delusion recreates reality around a person to make it less threatening to his or her self-centered (Sin) position. For example, it may seem obvious to everyone around that a teenager is an alcoholic, but the boy's mother denies the facts and relates to the boy as if he hardly drank at all—even if he's convicted of driving while intoxicated or goes to prison. Because of her need to be the best of mothers she "recreates" reality by blaming the boy's plight on judgmental teachers or police who "have it in for kids." She minimizes his drinking, even ignoring the scientific result of breath or blood tests.

Similar examples of delusion can be found in the unreal attitudes of a battered wife who says her husband "isn't so bad" (after the husband has broken her arm and burned her with cigarettes), or in the way adults sometimes refuse to see faults in their parents even when the parents abused them emotionally, physically, or even sexually and simply "weren't there for them" when they were young.

And the Disease has caused us to develop all kinds of subtle conscious and unconscious ways of "forgetting" embarrassing failures and sins in our personal lives. I have made promises to people close to me that I would be home on time, take them somewhere, fix something, set aside some time to talk about an issue important to them—and failed to do so. When confronted I have often denied I promised to do whatever it was—and often I really couldn't remember. But before I saw the denial in my life I would assume *they* were wrong about my promise if I couldn't remember.

At one level the process of denial is a matter of spiritual survival, since we are born with a sensitivity to the moral responsibilities we have and we *must* see ourselves in some way as OK, or even righteous, in order to accept ourselves. So we learn to rationalize instantly and creatively the moment a conflict comes up. If, for instance, my wife asks why I did something that appears to be insensitive and not very intelligent (like buying a very expensive luxury item after telling her, "We *have to economize severely!*") the Disease causes my mind to jump immediately to my defense with a "logical reason" that is calculated to make me look more sensible but may have had nothing at all to do with my decision at the time of the purchase. For instance, I might remind my wife that my aunt gave me some money two years before to "get something for myself." And "since she is coming to visit this spring I thought it would be an insult to her if I hadn't honored her request in two years. So I bought it." And once I said this, it would become true for me— even though the real truth was that in the presence of my greed I had denied to myself our pact to economize in order to get the thing I wanted. My aunt's request had not even crossed my mind—until I was challenged.

The tragedy is that denial and delusion build walls between us and God, between us and other people, and between us and the part of ourselves we want most to be. The self-deception forces us into a life of sinning that we can't even see. Potentially we may become self-righteous and, like the whited sepulchers Jesus spoke of, never know it. This is a frightening prospect.

To Present a Realistic Picture, We Make "Exceptions"

The Disease of Sin is so tricky that we may even admit one sin in order to cover up another more threatening one. And since we *are* conscious of many of our sins and feelings, such honesty in "admitting faults" makes it especially difficult to see the ones we are repressing.

There are certain areas in which we will "let ourselves see" the conflict. For instance, if I am tempted to do something dishonest financially (like cheat on my income tax or an expense account), for me the dilemma is likely to be in full view. I may wrestle with this briefly, but I am so committed to being an honest person that I would seldom actually do something dishonest financially (although I have rationalized and done this too).

Since I have many such areas in which I *can* allow myself to view the conflicts and follow through with appropriate moral and ethical decisions, I honestly believed that I was dealing with all my "sins"—or at least that I was aware of them. And since I had so many areas of honesty to point to, I felt that I was an honest man.

But inside each of us in our self-centered control room are areas that are deeply and unconsciously tied to our ultimate security. And these are often the areas in which Sin attacks us most insidiously through denial. Although I was almost always honest financially, unconsciously I was using some of my compulsions (like those pertaining to work, intensity, alcohol, and people) to hide my self-centered feelings from myself as I manipulated and tried to control those with whom I lived and worked, whose love and affirmation were crucial to me.

This kind of controlling is very difficult to describe, since it is often invisible to the controller *and* sometimes to people witnessing it—although they may feel uneasy watching the relationship between the one controlled and the controller.

One can be a very controlling person and not know it because of being in denial. A good friend of mine was amazed at what he discovered about his relationship with his sons. He gave me permission to write this. He put it this way: "From my point of view I've always been a nonjudgmental guy who gives the people around me a lot of room to be themselves. And I really resent people who try to run their families' lives and tell 'em what to do all the time.

"I didn't see myself as critical of my boys. Oh, occasionally I'd see them do something dumb and talk to them about it. What I didn't know—until this week—was that they see me as *totally* controlling. My kids just told me that they're *afraid of me*! Can you imagine that? I never knew it. And for years they've tried to do things the way they think I'd do 'em—to avoid the hassle of me straightening them out. But they said that when they do something in a way I *wouldn't* do it (something "dumb" from my perspective), all hell breaks loose, and I jump all over them.

"And I always saw myself as helping them with 'common sense suggestions.' Because they're so scared of my fast-draw criticism, they feel controlled both when I'm *not* complaining (but watching them) and when I *am* complaining. But from *my* perspective all I've known is that most of the time things are going fine and they're being 'rational and smart kids' (by doing what I'd do). Every once in a while when they foul up I am there with friendly counsel and advice. But from *their* perspective my advice isn't rare or friendly. They say I've got a hell of a load of anger I can't see, which I dump on them. In fact they say that I'm trying to run their lives, but that I don't even know I'm doing it. And you know, I never saw it before, but they're right. I go nuts when they do stupid things—things I wouldn't do."

This is a very painful sort of thing for a parent to admit. But I can sure identify with it. And I know now that when a man's kids or spouse claim that he is controlling or manipulating, and he is not conscious of doing these things, he *may be* in denial. The Disease may be making his family or business associates absolutely miserable through him without his ever knowing it. I am convinced that many divorces and many "runaways" by children are caused by this kind of denied manipulating and control—control that the perpetrator never sees. The controlling parent is angry at the crazy or ungrateful kids who "won't listen to anybody" and feels confused because he or she has an unreasonable spouse or a child who's "paranoid."

In my case I was seldom confronted about my controlling ways. Many people who are able to demonstrate a lot of honest, loving, and generous behavior are considered to be rigorously honest. People who attack them are considered to be cranks or ungrateful. Besides, the Sin-disease has such a hold on our society now that to talk to someone openly—even in the heart of the Christian fellowship—about inconsistencies between his or her behavior and expressed beliefs is considered meddling and judging and can be met with defensive hostility.

When people close to me questioned my behavior I was usually willing to consider calmly what they might be saying. (I was always *consciously* ready to learn the truth about myself.) But since I often couldn't "see" the selfish motive in my life they were pointing to, I could not honestly agree that they were right and begin to change. Instead, I rationalized my behavior and wound up being irritated at *them* for "misjudging" my motives. And my denied motives were especially hard to catch—even by me—since I was willing and able to own so many imperfections. People around me sometimes got very frustrated. They knew something was wrong, but they couldn't pin it down—and neither could I.

We Lose the Healing Power of Our Feelings

Our feelings constitute a wonderful "warning system" that tells us when we need to focus on a certain danger area in our lives or something that needs our love and attention. These feelings can activate energy and guidance to keep us safe, to heal our hurts, and to help us follow our highest ideals. But when we are in denial we bury these feelings, push them into our unconscious like pushing giant beach balls under water. We then don't experience our feelings clearly, so we can't heed their signals and take care of ourselves. We may feel mostly numbness or vague anxiety, and the creative, healing energy attached to our feelings sours and becomes destructive as we repress it under pressure. And when a feeling does get loose it comes up with exaggerated force "at an angle" and may hurt someone, like a beach ball that has been pushed far under water and finally pops to the surface.

But our feelings are our friends if we can learn how to let them happen and listen to them.

Anger

For example, many religious people think that the act of experiencing anger is somehow sinful. They take pride in almost never being angry. (I was one of these.) But a check of the Bible indicates that *God* was angry much of the time throughout the Hebrews' history. There are many, many references to his being angry enough to destroy people (e.g., Josh. 7:10–26; Ezek. 14:6–11).

Of course it is also written (with some relief, I suspect) that God is one who is slow to anger. And throughout the Bible we read that anger is very powerful and we should be slow to anger (e.g., Eccles. 7:9). But evil really angers God, and his anger is kindled against Sin and sinful people a lot. In the New Testament, Jesus got very angry (e.g., Mark 3:5).

If the God of Israel in the Old Testament and Jesus in the New were angry to the point of violent action (see Mark 11:15–19), then anger in itself must not be evil. To act out our anger to hurt or abuse helpless people or manipulate them for our own satisfaction is not what I am talking about. Those are harmful behaviors. That anger often falls under the heading of "rage," or uncontrollable anger.

But the *feeling* of anger can be a powerful and creative experience. Anger can provide energy, strength, and for many of us, courage we don't normally have to stand up against our own Sin and the evil that people want to do to us or others. We are advised by Paul to use anger against evil: "Hate what is evil" (Rom. 12:9). Anger at evil and injustice has provided much of the energy for the creative social changes in every era.

If we are not in touch with our anger, we lose the value and strength of anger, which could give us the motivation to begin to deal with Sin in our world or in our own lives.

For example, I knew a man who was an alcoholic but couldn't see that he had a problem with drinking—although his wife was on the verge of leaving him since he was drunk and out of control almost every night and many days. Finally the man got in a serious automobile accident while drunk and the judge gave him the alternative of going to prison or going to a chemical dependency treatment center. The man felt no guilt and thought the judgment was unfair. But he went to the treatment center.

When he got there he was still in denial about his alcoholism and wouldn't participate in the program honestly or face his feelings. His cocky know-it-all attitude and his continued refusal to look at his own feelings got him kicked out of the treatment center.

He was enraged! He'd show them he could get sober! And it was his anger that motivated him and produced the energy to focus on his problem. When he got back into treatment he saw that he was an alcoholic and got into AA and worked through a strong program of recovery.

Fear

Although compulsive fear based on projection can be harmful and debilitating, our experience of fear in the face of real present danger or threat can be a wise guide. If we can be in touch with our fear when we are about to do something immoral or something harmful to ourselves, then we may see the wisdom of that fear, which can keep us from doing the harmful or sinful thing. Our fear can become our wisdom. Many counselees have told me that they were about to make a bad business decision or to have an illicit affair that might have wrecked their lives when they were struck by a wave of fear that made them stop and see what they were doing and helped them make a wise decision.

Pain

Our pain can help us if we don't repress it. If I have been hurt by another person or by the death of someone I love and deny the pain, it will fester inside me and isolate me in ways I do not understand. Anger often comes to cover my pain, and I get irritable and strike out at the very people who could comfort me and help me through the pain I am repressing. But if I *feel* and *express* the pain, I can confess it openly to God and my brothers and sisters in God's family of recovering sinners. He and they can help me bear the pain and come out again into health on the other side of the injury or grief.

I have a friend who was betrayed by his business partner. The scandal, which had some bizarre aspects to it, became public knowledge in a "front page" way. My friend, who is a counselor, felt the pain, the disappointment, and the anger at his partner. And in feeling the pain he got in touch with painful feelings of betrayal he had experienced as a child at the hands of his mother, anger that had been long repressed. Although the whole experience was no fun, my friend was healed and became a much stronger and freer person as a result of letting himself feel his anger and pain.

The Self-sufficient, "Victorious" Trap

But if we stuff our fears and other feelings and try to build a reputation for having strong faith or being self-sufficient by claiming proudly that we don't have feelings like fear, anger, and grief, sooner or later it becomes expedient for us to repress more and more of our feelings about certain threatening areas. We must deny these feelings so that we can maintain our sense of "being fine, adequate people" or "dedicated and victorious Christians" in the face of the very real feelings, problems, and behaviors that might contradict that fantasy. We may unconsciously isolate ourselves from the guidance of our feelings, from those who are experiencing life and could help us, and from God.

Since most of this process of denial is unconscious, any good religious man, for instance, can have a hidden side and be a thoughtless husband and father, or even an insensitive or abusive tyrant, to his wife and family and never face it consciously. Or he can rationalize his tyranny as "necessary" for "helping" his wife and family "get in line with God's will." (Of course, a wife can do the same, or can be a controlling manipulator who always acts put upon and denies the ways she runs the family through indirect manipulation.)

Bad Public Relations with the World

Denial and delusion often make us baffling to people outside the church. They know that we who claim to be God's people are supposed to have peace and joy and are supposed to behave with love and rigorous honesty. But then they see that some of us are insensitive and unloving to our families or dishonest in business (another area of denial for some people) or in other areas of our lives. And yet we profess the faith with "clear consciences" and are active "in church every Sunday."

People who don't understand about denial think

that we *know* that we are doing these inconsistent and dishonest things. For years this was very confusing to me, but now it seems apparent that in those cases the Sin-disease is operating successfully in another of us Christians. How then do we break through this denial and get to a place where we can see and deal with the ravages of Sin in our lives?

The truth is that in various stages we are all in the grips of the disease of Sin (Rom. 3:23). "If we say we have no sin, we deceive ourselves, and the truth is not in us" (1 John 1:8) And since by ourselves we cannot even *see*, much less change, many of our denied sinful motives and behaviors, we are powerless on our own to get well.

Our self-centered trying to be first or number one or "right" in our family, our vocational life, and our other relationships leads us to the lonely, resentful, and fearful isolation for which the world has no cure. And if by some chance we can control our *conscious* tendencies to commit the more blatant sins (murder, adultery, or stealing, for example), we will deviously work out our self-centered desires by denying to consciousness our strategies to control other people and take God's place in our small circle of influence. We will live in a delusion of righteousness while we cause havoc in the lives of others.

Finally we may become confused and at our wits' end, since we are trying to overcome our problems but are still miserable. There is in us a strong continuing and *increasing* urge to do and say things that foul our own nests, until we are frantic with fear and confusion. It's as if there is an honest part of us trapped inside who is determined to let the secret of our denial out even if it means sabotaging the carefully built exterior image. Paul described his confusing dilemma this way: "I of myself serve the law of God with my mind, but with my flesh [the urgent, unconscious part] I serve the law of sin" (Rom. 7:25). And in this same context Paul cries out our cry when we see our powerlessness to make things right on our own, "Wretched man that I am! Who will deliver me from this body of death?" (Rom. 7:24).

10

To the End of Ourselves

If we are fortunate, that moment finally comes when we are sick and tired of the confusion and anxiety, of the guilt, the fear of the future and/or death. We realize that we are powerless on our own to "fix life up" for ourselves and other people.

The problem seems to be, as one writer put it, that

each person is like an actor who wants to run the whole show; is forever trying to manage the lights, the ballet, the scenery and the rest of the players in his own way. If his arrangements would only stay put, if only people would do as he wishes, the show would be great. Everybody, including himself, would be pleased. Life would be wonderful. In trying to make these arrangements our actor may sometimes be quite virtuous. He [or she] may be kind, considerate, patient, generous; even modest and self-sacrificing. On the other hand, he may be mean, egotistical, selfish and dishonest. But as with most humans, he is likely to have varied traits.

What usually happens? The show doesn't come off very well. He begins to think life doesn't treat him right. He decides to exert himself more. He becomes, on the next occasion, still more demanding or gracious, as the case may be. Still the play does not suit him. Admitting he may be somewhat at fault, he is sure that other people are more to blame. He becomes angry, indignant, self-pitying. What is his basic trouble? Is he not really a self seeker even when trying to be kind? Is he not a victim of the delusion that he can wrest satisfaction and happiness out of this world if he only manages well? Is it not evident to all the rest of the players that these are the things he wants? And do not his actions make each of them wish to retaliate, snatching all they can get out of the show? Is he not, even in his best moments, a producer of confusion rather than harmony?[1]

Indeed we are all, it seems, sinners. And that means we are at some level deeply self-centered—though we may hide that fact behind good deeds or (as in my case) behind a flourishing Christian ministry. And in our attempts to direct the drama of which we are a part (either subtly or openly), we are filled with many forms of fear, self-delusion, resentment, and self-pity as we manipulate people and they retaliate. They hurt us in seemingly unreasonable ways, but usually (if we could but remember) we have hurt them sometime in the past. In any case we wind up unhappy, confused, and feeling misunderstood, because we cannot see behind the walls of our denial.

God's Power Comes When We Give Up on Ours

At this point we are dealing with power, pure and simple. We do not *have* the power to defeat Sin alone and put God back in the center of our lives. What can we do? Some people cry out to God in their sense of powerlessness and ask him to help them. And they are very disappointed when he doesn't. But there is a paradox here. Apparently, until we *give up on our power* and agendas and turn our lives and our wills over to him, we cannot experience or use the power of God to overcome Sin in our lives. We must, it seems, surrender.

I realize that people may come into a valid relationship with God in all kinds of ways: gradually, violently, as children or as adults. Some come because they see the beauty of nature, the creative activity of God, and they want to worship him. Others come through an intellectual search for meaning. But as valid as these motives of attraction may be, none of them helped me deal with my Sin. If others have received the power of God to overcome the Sin-disease in their lives, I rejoice with them.

But for me, and for thousands of other people who have faced the power of Sin in their lives, there had to be more. We who have been so afraid of *really* turning loose and abandoning our lives into the hands of God had to walk the way I am about to describe (or something like it).

First, after trying in every way we could think of to solve the problems our Sin caused us, we had to consciously realize our powerlessness. Then we had to make a specific act of surrender or decision to turn our will and our lives over to the care of God. These steps are the only way we have become able to use the power of God to overcome the Disease in our lives.

The way the surrender takes place may be different for each person, but certain events seem to "mark the trail" for almost everyone.

What I'm going to say in this chapter and the next may be old hat to you. If you have read other books by me you may have seen elements of this discussion. But I feel I must talk about surrender in light of the Sin-disease here, because only if one grasps what is involved in a life-opening surrender to God does the rest of this book make sense.

All Have Sinned—A Review of the Process of Surrender

The universal nature of Sin is such that without ever knowing it *all* of us become centered in ourselves in a way that is not conducive to healthy relationships and to long-term happiness. We put ourselves in the center where only God belongs. The way this Sin often manifests itself is that we gradually begin to focus on one thing in particular in our lives so much that eventually we cannot by our own strength want God more than that thing. Since denial is operating, we don't see the extent to which our lives are being absorbed by whatever is capturing them (by promising to make us feel good or make us OK). Our attention can be captured this way by a chemical or other addictive substance, sex, gambling, or criminal habits. Or what we focus on can be something that is *good* in itself; it doesn't have to be a "bad" thing. For instance, this focus may be on a behavior, like work, or on another person, a mate, for instance, or a child, or it can be on religious programs or ourselves and our own ambitions. But whatever this unhealthy, compulsive attention is focused on, *that* is the controlling manifestation of our own particular Sin.

Although we are not *conscious* that we are so intently focused on one area of our lives, the amount of time and attention we give that hottest area of our thoughts gives us away. And this thing that we put in the center of our living to satisfy us can become an idol, replacing God as the security and center of our lives.

As long as things are going well in the area of our Sin-security, we feel important and in control. But sooner or later putting something or someone in the center of one's life, where only God belongs, leads a sensitive person to the end of his or her rope. Evidently nothing will give us the safety and power of God in our lives, except God. When we overfocus our lives upon anything or any relationship that is not God, sooner or later we spoil it, and it will fail us. For, in fact, we are not in control of life, and no thing or person can meet our deepest needs for security and fulfillment.

Awakened by a Personal Crisis

This realization of powerlessness sometimes occurs with a personal or vocational crisis. Such a crisis may be brought about by illness, death of someone close, errors in judgment, an "unrepairable" confrontation with a loved one, or being caught at a specific, undeniable sin. A rush of shame and fear may come when it becomes apparent that one is powerless to "fix things up" or to hide the problem. This anxiety can be acute and may feel like being in a fog of fear, loneliness, failure, and guilt. Much of our seeking after money, power, fame, or pleasure is evidently to provide security against being caught off guard and shown to be inadequate and not the "powerful one" at all. We must keep reassuring ourselves, because at one level we know that we cannot trust the "God of ourselves."

Throughout this process our Sin tries to get us to "deny" that we are putting anything in God's place or that we are powerless to handle the situation. This is evidently because when we see and confess our Sin we can repent, surrender, put God back in the center, and *defeat the Disease*—thus overcoming the alienated, guilty feeling that things are not OK. And when God is in place in the center of our lives, then we have his power to confront and deal with the continuing insidious and addictive force of the Disease.

Some Common Examples of the Sin-Disease in Action

It seems to work like this: If, for instance, a man decides that his goal is to build a business, he may start out with a normal desire to succeed. But somewhere along the line, succeeding becomes identified in his mind with his very worth as a person—though he may deny this at a conscious level. Instead of enjoying his family and the beautiful natural things God has put around him, his vision becomes completely focused on his work.

Gradually all his creative time and energy is devoted to building and maintaining his business. When he is at home, he may be distant, preoccupied, and unrelated emotionally to what he's doing with his family. Sitting in the center of his life with his business, he can only see that he *must* succeed.

He may have to sacrifice moral and ethical principles. He can become tense and overanxious and blow the business by bad judgment. Or he may ruin his family and leave his friends along the way—winding up "successful" but lonely and isolated. Whenever we become the center of our lives, where only God belongs, we wind up destroying part of the beauty and wonder of the life and relationships God has given us to cultivate and to enjoy.

Overfocused Parenting

Another example has to do with the wonderful gift of being a parent and having the opportunity to raise a child for God until he or she is an adult. When a mother, for instance, makes the child the "most important thing in her life," the center, then the Disease can really go to town on destroying that family.

Although this may be shocking to some, when a parent makes a child the center of his or her life, where only God should be, it is a form of idolatry that the Sin-disease seems to revel in. For years things may be manageable, in that the child may be "behaving" and making the mother proud. She feels important and in control. Being a parent is a happy experience, even if it is difficult and demanding at times.

But then things change, perhaps in adolescence, and the child begins to do and say things the mother doesn't approve of and can't comprehend. Anxiety and fear start to fill the mother's life. Thoughts and even prayers about the child take up every minute.

Although to the mother this may seem to be "normal concern," as the tension mounts the parent becomes obsessed by the child's behavior. This obsession with fixing the child to be the way she wants him or her to be can easily become the central focus of the mother's life—instead of God. Because of denial the mother may not realize that she is manipulating and trying to dominate the child's life. She feels that all she is doing is "for the child's own good." I have lived in this delusion for years as a parent.

The mother tries everything she knows to "straighten the child out." Nothing works. She becomes absorbed by fear, loneliness, a sense of failure, hurt, resentment, guilt, and loss of meaning.

Help is enlisted to change the child. Teachers, counselors, ministers, doctors may be brought in, but nothing works. Then, perhaps after many tears and much fear, the mother may become horrified to realize that she is powerless over the child.

The process is similar if the focus of one's life is on something else—alcohol, sex, or pleasing people, for example. The progression is similar. At first, the alcohol, for instance, is for "fun." But then, sooner or later, it becomes the master and the "fun" is replaced by fear.

When this point is reached there seems to be no way out. Everything that we know and possess won't make things right. We are alone inside in our frantic state, and powerless.

11

The First Movement
Toward Surrender

When the frenzy and pain become strong enough and the frantic person realizes that he or she is powerless to reconcile business and family, or powerless over a child, a mate, or a chemical, there may be a crisis point at which the businessman, or mother, decides that whatever the cost he or she has got to change something—the agony is too much.

Let's say such a person hears the good news of God's offer to accept us just as we are, to restore us to sanity from our Sin, our frantic strivings to succeed or to change people, places, and things to suit our plans.

When we admit that we are powerless over the Sin-disease (our selfishness and its consequences) we have taken the first step toward healing, joy, peace, and a new experience of living.[1] The next step is to believe that God can and will change our lives and restore us to a sane, balanced view of our relationships (in spite of all the pain and damage caused by our Sin).

When we believe that, we are ready to take the third step, which is to surrender, to abandon our lives and our wills to God as we understand him at that time. But at this point a great struggle may begin.

Surrendering the control panel of our lives to God is about the hardest thing we can do, and unless the alternative is to lose something we are not prepared to live without (like our sanity, freedom, peace of mind, family), only a rare person will do it.

Is It Possible to Turn Loose?

To someone who has never considered this step it looks hard—impossible, in fact. How can one actually turn one's life over to God? How can a reasonable person "turn loose" control of his or her life? But as is the case with so much of the life of faith, we get help from another Source than our own willpower—from the other side of the surrender we are contemplating. One person said that the decision about surrendering is like facing a locked door. All we need to get beyond it is a key and the decision to walk through the door. "There is only one key, and it is called willingness. Once unlocked by willingness, the door opens almost of itself, and looking through it, we shall see a pathway beside which is an inscription. It reads: 'This is the way to a faith that works.'"[2] We may shut the door later because of our Sin, but it will always open again the moment we are ready to use the key of willingness. Having said this, however, deciding to turn one's life over to God, or even being willing to, still may bring on an agonizing struggle if a person understands what is at stake.

The Struggle to Surrender

In the agony of the situation leading to this point, we may finally decide to quit trying to fix things by ourselves, and turn loose. In the mother's case that might mean realizing that she is ready to turn all of her life over to God. She realizes that she is powerless to control the child's life and is ready to stop trying to change the child. What is often happening at this point is that by being ready to surrender to God we are also surrendering to life on life's terms, instead of trying to make people, life, and God live on our terms.

This does not mean that the mother comes to God to get him to straighten the *child* out. It evidently won't work that way. Each person must long to turn away from the sickness, the addiction, the discouragement and failure that has devastated his or her *own* life.

Some people say that they have tried this, and it didn't work. But when I ask them about that, it usually turns out that they have tried to commit the child— the problem—to God *without* surrendering their *own* lives and futures to him. Others offer their lives to God *if* he will straighten out their child—or problem. That is bartering with God and evidently won't work either.

One has to realize that one's *own* life is unmanageable and surrender it *all* to God, asking only for help to learn his will and for the strength to do it. I have found no way to bypass this process. And the by-products of this commitment are often startling. When, for instance, a parent surrenders this way he or she may be able to release the child—incidentally freeing the child to develop the independent life God has for him or her.

The attempt at total commitment is necessary from the sufferer's perspective because sinners can't afford to *see* their Sin and character defects until or unless they can see that they will be given the power to *deal with* this denied Sin by the One to whom the surrender is being made. Otherwise the fear of failing and/or being—or appearing to be—worthless will force us to keep our blinders on. We are afraid that if we give up what control we have, we may not be seen as anything of value to those we love. Then we would be lost indeed—or so we feel.

The Myth of Control

You may be saying, "That's all very well for people who *are* powerless and out of control, but my life certainly isn't unmanageable." I certainly wouldn't argue with you about that. I didn't think I was powerless either. But for me, "control" was different from what I had thought it was.

When I was a small boy I remember my mother and father arguing at the dinner table. I was frightened and prayed fervently that they would quit.

Somehow I got the idea at that time that *I* could change *their* feelings for each other to positive, loving ones if I could just talk to them, love them enough, or be good or "outstanding" enough in school or out in the world. I didn't make a conscious decision that I could change their behavior by this sort of manipulation, but I must have felt that way, because whenever they had angry arguments I tried to be a "better boy" and make life more pleasant so they would quit fighting and stay together (and with me).

I suppose the fact that they did stay together and keep getting over their fights (for whatever reason) was how the myth of my being able to manipulate other people's feelings got its start. I thought I'd been a key factor in making it happen, but I know now that no one can change another in a positive direction. All we can do at best is influence others. *They* must decide to change *on their own* when the change relates to their own Sin-position. Yet the myth of control is an almost universal delusion, and it causes much pain in relationships.

By the time a man, for example, is grown and ready to marry he may think his spouse-to-be has some rough edges but that he can change her if he is just nice enough to her and loves her in the right way. After all, this often worked when they were dating, or so it seemed. But usually something goes wrong with that theory right after the wedding.

At first, when his wife doesn't change, the husband figures he wasn't doing the right thing or wasn't doing it correctly. So he redoubles his efforts. Later he thinks he wasn't being nice *enough*, so he becomes either sickening with his "niceness" or angry and demanding with his expectations. But those tactics don't work either. Neither way causes the desired change.

He may then try expensive gifts, trips, vacation

houses, on one hand, or isolation, infidelity, or physical abuse, on the other. But he still isn't able to change this person he married into his vision of what she could ("should") be. He may conclude that he has married an impossible, hardheaded woman who can't see reason (*his* reason) and divorce her. Or she may change outwardly but resent him intensely.

During this whole time the husband usually doesn't question the idea, that he's had since childhood, that he has the power to cause people to change and be what he thinks they ought to be.

He may see himself as a loving person who wants only the best for his family. He's baffled that his wife resents his suggestions. In his Sin he doesn't see that the "best things" from his wife's perspective may well be better for her than the "best things" *he* sees for her. (Of course, all this is applicable to women's attempts to change their husbands also—though tactics may be different from one person to another.)

When children come along the father may feel that here at last are people he can "help" (control). He wants to give *them* the best that he has as a father. But when his children are grown he often discovers that they too resented his attempts to change them into the people he thought God wanted them to be. He is genuinely surprised that he hasn't been able to do this. After all, he was grown and powerful when his children were born, and his intentions were "for *their* good."

Often it isn't until we fail or are rejected by the child or mate we are trying to change (or until we fail publicly and unmistakably to control a compulsive or addictive behavior) that we may realize that control of other people's motivations and of addictive behaviors is a myth. Even then, we may *still* try to deny that we have a problem we can't handle. The Disease is tricky and powerful indeed.

Such a failure is shattering but can act as a shaft of light by which God can show us the nature of the Sin inside our lives and its cunning tactics of denial, delusion, and grandiosity. We may see that our supposed power, or assumed right, to change other people—even for their own good—is a Sin-inspired illusion.

My friend Pia Mellody points out that any behavior we do automatically—without intending to—is behavior over which we are powerless (e.g., a resentment, or telling a mate or child what they should do).

Thomas Merton said that the beginning of love is to let those we love be perfectly themselves, and not to twist them to fit our own image. Otherwise we love only the reflection of ourselves we find in them. Under full sail I had set out on a course to "make my family happy," but I couldn't see that I was trying to make them behave as *I* would, to have the happiness *I* would have wanted were I in their shoes. Fortunately they wanted to live their own lives and find the happiness God put in their own imaginations.

For many of us, only our failure to be able to control important people, places, things, and addictive behaviors or substances in our lives can lead us to a place where we're ready to admit we are powerless and to commit our lives to God. Only then are we able to ask him for the motivation and power to see the denied reality of our lives and clean them up.

And if we turn our will and our lives over to the care of God as we understand him, we pass through

a portal to a new way of living. We can obtain un-
qualified forgiveness for our past (1 John 1:9) and
power and vision with which to attack the Disease. We
are forgiven by God for our controlling self-centeredness, our playing his role. He gives us new eyes, a new
meaning, and a simple program for living.

This new direction or goal is to find and do the will
of the loving God of the Bible. And the by-products
of this adventure are personal reformation and serenity.

Hobart Mower, once elected president of the American Psychological Association, to whom this change
came late in life said,

> So long as a person lives under the shadow of real,
> unacknowledged, and unexpiated guilt, he ... will
> continue to hate himself and to suffer the inevitable
> consequences of self-hatred. But the moment he ...
> begins to accept his guilt and his sinfulness, the pos-
> sibility of radical reformation opens up; and ... a new
> freedom of self-respect and peace.[3]

As Total a Surrender as We Can Make

All this begins as we decide to give control of our
lives and wills to God. This deciding represents as
total a commitment as we can honestly make to as
much of God as we can understand—however little
that may be. We may have to begin by only being able
to give God permission to place in us the *desire* to
surrender it all to him. But he will evidently accept
us at whatever level we can honestly give ourselves to

him. At this point I am convinced that the theological content of our commitment is not as important as the inner act of surrendering to God, who loves us and forgives us and can guide us toward healing and wholeness.

In any case this "deciding" is only a verbal step. The "surrendering" itself is a "living" process of turning loose to God that takes place from now on as we live one step at a time, trying to discover God's will and confronting the disease of Sin.

One of the striking things I see happening among those who are trying to recover from Sin and fight the Disease is that through the process I'm describing they wind up more well than they were before their Sin got them into trouble.

12

The End of a Long Road, and a New Beginning

There came a time when I was finally so burned out and tired of being frustrated and afraid that I was ready to get some help. I had been spending some time at a healing center out West in the midst of a community of caring people.

It was dawn after a sleepless night of struggling unsuccessfully. Sometime in the dark, hours before dawn, my denial had cracked open, and I really saw how much I had hurt people in my life and how I had excluded much, if not most, of my Sin-diseased behavior from my consciousness. The feelings of guilt and fear were overwhelming—and I felt so surprised! I had had no idea how manipulative and controlling I'd been in trying to be "right" and have things go the way I wanted them.

I was stuck in the center where only God should be. I had felt powerless before I made my first serious commitment to God on a roadside in Texas in 1956, but I had *never* seen the raw, naked strength and pervasiveness of my own Sin and felt the evil it had caused in me. And I knew I was helpless to face it alone.

When I turned to God that dawn I spoke to him haltingly and with a sense almost of terror and of acute need I couldn't remember having experienced before. All I could remember clearly about God that morning was that he was stronger than my Sin, and without him I knew I was lost.

As the pink-orange light of early morning lined the dark mountains across the valley from where I'd spent the night, I spoke to God. "I have tried to take your place and have hurt the people I love through my intense self-centeredness, God. I ask your forgiveness, and I surrender my whole life and my future to you. Please show me your will for my life, and give me the strength to do it."

That day I wandered around in a daze. I wept a lot—relief. Oh, I was relieved. I had given up trying to figure out how to heal myself and change my bad habits and compulsive behaviors. And I kept saying over and over, "I surrender it all to you. Show me how to live this hour." Then I would relax and weep again with gratitude for the relief from the awful struggle to control, to change, to keep from admitting *I* was the problem. It was suddenly obvious to me that my self-centeredness and need to be right and to be considered adequate had kept me bound up in my disease, with its compulsions and fears.

I was afraid, because I didn't know how to live without my compulsions and my controlling and manipulative habits. All that day I felt shy and awkward with people, because what I had just seen coming through the cracks of my denial made me realize that I didn't know who I really was at all.

But at the same time it was as if a calm voice inside me said, "Don't worry. *I* know who you are and I'll show you. Just relax and trust me." And I shook my head as I realized that I *had* to trust God to show me the way now, because I didn't have the first idea what was going to happen to me.

In the days and weeks that followed my dawn surrender I didn't want to impress God or get him to help me "become something for him," or even make the things right I'd fouled up. I just wanted him to show me his will for each day. If I did that, I felt the rest would follow. I knew that I was dealing with the creator of the universe, but I also knew that in all his majesty he has been revealed to us as an intimate Father.

In other words, although I was now seeing God as awesome, powerful, and distant, I also realized with a sharp sense of gratitude that I had been invited to come close to him, close enough that he could hear the faintest frightened whisper of my aching heart. And in a new way I've come to believe that he *cares*—as I care for my children when they are suffering. I have often wept tears of gratitude as it has come over me what that caring means to me now.[1] I can talk to him as I would love to have talked to my own father but was afraid to. I can reveal *anything* of myself to him (even those awful and fearful thoughts and actions I have discovered behind my walls of denial and delusion—which I didn't ever want to tell anyone).

In a gradual, transrational way he is becoming more real to me—though not in the "casual, friendly" way the relationship used to appear. I had known God "personally" before, but I had not seen him as the awesome Mighty One—the God of justice—who is waging war on principalities and powers and who wrestles evil in us every night and day for the saving of our "here and now" lives from the clutches of our own Sin. I saw that God loved me as I was, but also that he was expecting me to change and deal with the effects of my Sin.

Standing on Solid Ground

I remembered reading a newspaper story years ago about three men who were out duck hunting on a cold December morning. They all were wearing waist-high rubber waders. On the way to the blind the small flatbottomed boat capsized, and the men were thrown into the cold water of the lake. After thrashing around trying to swim ashore, all the men drowned. The article pointed out that the accident was particularly tragic since the water where the boat had capsized was less than five feet deep—but the men did not know that. Had they not panicked, and if they had simply put their feet down, they would have been standing on solid ground.

I had felt a little like those men the past few years. I had been praying frantically while struggling with great effort to try to get out of the chaotic mess of my inner life. But I was struggling so hard to "do it myself" that in my lack of faith I didn't know how— or was afraid—to put my feet down and let my full weight rest on God.

Since that commitment at dawn I'm trying to "put my feet down." I don't "say" as much to God as I did before. I try to be aware of his presence and enjoy being quiet with him, just resting next to his solid strength and love as I do my work and walk through my days and nights. I'm not proposing this as the way others should live, but for me it has much meaning. As I am taking the steps necessary to stay in recovery from the Sin-disease I feel a more steady and concrete trust in God.

For me this way has meant a whole new approach to faith. Instead of thinking I can "figure out" how to solve my basic human problems, I now know that I can only show up each day and trust that if I turn my life over to God that day and do the simple things I am learning to do, he will show me enough to get me through the day and on toward whatever his will is for me tomorrow.

I'm happy and seeing signs of healing from the Disease. But this has meant a reorientation of my spiritual life and disciplines.

The Unseen Warfare Begins

When I began to live again after my confrontation and dawn surrender I was sobered to realize the power of the Disease over my life. I saw that the person committing his or her life to God's care has entered a life-and-death battle. And I was amazed at the amount of fear that is involved in this struggle for me. I sometimes wake up afraid that I won't *ever* be able to change and will wind up a failure, alone and rejected. These and other irrational fears are evidently par for the course in this spiritual battle.

For those of us who have denied our feelings for so long, they are often very strong when we start facing them in this struggle—even with God's help. But the battle is crucial. It is for the rebirth and development of the person God made (in potential) inside each of us.

Part of this battle is visible from the beginning. There are some things about my life that I can see that need changing, sins and character defects of which I am aware and have worried about for years. I can do battle openly with these crippling defects of character through confession and making amends.

As I tried to deal with those problems that had become "visible" in my life, God, over the months, began to show me more and more of the *hidden,* denied parts of me. I believe he would have me deal with these things as I can see them in order to become the person he made me to be. It might take the rest of my life, but I saw that I could at least make a small beginning. These are things that I now realize have been with me since I was a child. And I have seen that in one sense I must become a child again before God in order to rid myself of these defensive defects of character that have caused me to remain in my delusion of being the center and in control.

III

A Reorientation To Prayer, Bible Reading, and Worship in Light of the Sin-Disease

13

Personal Prayer: A Way Back to Intimacy with God

Authentic prayer often begins with cries for help. And by the nature of the dilemma of the recovering sinner, it should. When I realize I am powerless—and that I am not God at all—and then come in contact with One who *is* God, "Help!" may be the only sane prayer.

Since that dawn experience of my own, I have discovered several things that have helped me to stay alive spiritually and to open myself to God. My prayers have not been flowery or pretty, they are direct and simple. I ask him for help in the mornings to know and do his will. At night I thank him for getting me through another day and for what he has given me in it. After my years of studying various methods of praying used by the saints, my communication with God now seems almost stark in its simplicity.

"Can You Trust God for Twenty-four Hours?"

Someone asked me if I thought I could trust God with my life for one day only. I said, "Of course." He told me that that was all I ever had to do, because today is the only *real* time there is. So, after years of developing vast schemes and filling my creative present moments with worries about the future or guilt and shame (or remembered insults or victory scenes) of the past, I began again to concentrate on living in today only. (I'd done that years ago, but as the Sin-disease got worse I moved back into living in fearful and frustrating worlds of the future or the past.) To stay in "today" I would imagine that my world ended at eleven o'clock each night. If some worry came to mind about something that might happen in the future, or if I remembered a resentment from the past, I would tell that worry or resentment I wasn't interested in anything but today. I'd pick such worries up by the scruff of the neck like unruly puppies that had pooped on the carpet of my today, put them out, clean up the mess, and get back to the activity at hand.

It is still hard for me to give up the lifetime habit of worrying about the future and reliving the past. But I realized that my "todays" had been absolutely cluttered with anxious and debilitating feelings about the past and the future. I still make plans for the future, but then I quit picking at my plans and fantasizing failure. I list the things I can do today and trust him with the future. (Some days I have to do this many times a day.)

Since I had also been unconsciously needing to control the lives of those around me in order to "make them happy," I had worried about what was going to happen to *them* too in the future. I worried about my wife's life and happiness, my children's, and even some of my friends'. I sometimes felt like the lady in a story I heard recently: when she was dying, *someone else's* life flashed before her eyes. No wonder I hadn't known much peace and serenity!

Praying Yourself into Reality Each Day

My friend Fred Downing told me that when he got up each morning he used a simple prayer format to pull himself into the day before him. From his simple plan I have developed the following, which I use each morning:

1. I get up and thank God for *one specific thing or person*. That makes my faith specific, as I choose what I'm thankful for.
2. I commit my *whole life* to God, putting the past and future in his hands and specifically surrendering this particular day to him.

I soon discovered a discouraging fact. I would give God my "whole life" at 7 A.M. But by nine the same morning I would be very worried about a relationship or my financial future or a sick friend. And this let me know that I hadn't surrendered whatever it was I was worried about at all. If I trust God and give something to him, believing that he wants the best for that person or situation (and will teach me through whatever may happen), then any subsequent frantic anxiety is a dead giveaway that I haven't surrendered that issue to God at all. I am still trying to control whatever it is I am frantic about. I was discouraged, since I wanted to commit my life "perfectly" (more of my Sin).

A Spiritual Crud Detector

I saw that here is a great way to discover exactly what those things are in my life that I am not yet really willing to surrender to God. I began to list the things I worry about on a paper I keep with my devotional book. Although the list changes in "intensity" of emphasis, some of the people and things I have trouble releasing are my wife, my children, my financial life, my vocational life, my need to justify myself, and my self-centered fear of failure. Each day when I come to this section on surrendering my whole life to God, I tell him it is my intention to commit these things specifically—and I read my list. This has helped me to live in the present and to be more realistic, honest, and humble about my attempts to turn my *whole* life over to God.

3. I ask God to let me know his will for me for this particular day as the day goes along. I don't expect "voices," but I listen. And it is surprising how this attitude helps me to make better decisions about the use of my time than I did when I didn't keep his channel on. Sometimes I get clear indications of things I need to do. More

and more I am feeling comfortable with this process, even though I've made some mistakes and realized that what I thought was God's will in fact was not.

4. I ask God for the strength and courage to do his will this one day and to trust him with the outcome of my actions.

5. I name one person I am going to contact today by a personal visit, telephone call, or letter. I do this because I want to move out of my self-absorption and to thank God in this way for his love for me. The person I contact may be a relative or friend or someone I've wanted to know in our town. Or it may be someone who visited our church. By only listing *one* person I can stay realistically in today. If I can't reach that person, I try not to beat myself, but just wait and contact someone tomorrow. This is how I am beginning to give away the love I am receiving—which I have been assured is the only way this approach to life will work.

6. I read a segment in a daily devotional book and/or the Bible (see chapters 15 and 16 on Bible reading). I started out years ago with Oswald Chambers's *My Utmost for His Highest* and Thomas à Kempis's *Imitation of Christ,* but I have recently been through *One Day at a Time* and Phil Parham's *Letting God.* I have read dozens of others over the years.

This simple prayer format is flexible regarding time. And being specific and not overloading it has been key to sharpening my focus on God and on real people in today.

A New Sort of Praying

Many mornings I wake up afraid, but I use the simple format I have just described. All through the day I catch myself at times being aware that I have hope in God. When this happens I say, "Thank you, God," and ask him to show me his will for the rest of the day. When I start to get frantic, I confess to God that I am powerless to quit being frantic and that my life is unmanageable. Then I make a decision to turn my life and my will over to him and get back to work. For me, this works really well much of the time—though I may have to call someone to talk about my feelings before I can get back to work with any serenity.

At Night

At night I think back through the day to see if I have been hurting myself and other people through the character defects I have denied for so long. I sort of take a mini-inventory of the areas of my life that lead me into Sin-diseased thinking. And I recall the good things that have happened during the day.

First I ask myself if I indulged in:

Self-pity ("Poor me, they are not treating *me* right—after all *I've* done for them," etc.)

Self-justification ("You don't understand. I had a *good reason* for what I did! Listen...")

Self-righteousness ("I do better than most people. And my motives are good. I pray a lot and work in church and write books. I'm surprised that this person is angry with me.")

Self-will ("Why can't that stupid jerk *move* that car? The light changed ten minutes ago!" Or, "I don't need any help from *anyone*. I can do it by myself.")

Selfishness ("I'm sorry I'm too busy to help now, but give me another chance," or—with a long, disappointed face—"Sorry you're tired and not feeling well, but I'd just hoped we could go out tonight.")

Dishonesty ("I'd *love* to come, but there is no way I could make it Tuesday.")

Resentment ("That's not fair! After all I've done for that———, and he's not even being honest with me!")

Fear ("What if no one buys my new book! I'll starve!")

At night I try not to dwell on the mistakes of the day but just confess them to God and make a note to make amends to people if that's appropriate. After taking this mini-inventory of character defects I list in my mind those *good* things that have happened during the day (e.g., felt good, did my prayer time and went for a walk, enjoyed lunch with Glen and Bill, got some work accomplished on my book, had a good visit with Lynn, enjoyed the lecture tonight on personality types by Richard Grant, at the lecture enjoyed the visit with three friends I haven't seen in ten years, had a close time with Andrea on the way home). I am always surprised at how many good things have happened—when I look for them.

When I have finished this brief recounting of the day I turn the past day over to God and go to sleep. By taking this inventory each night, I am not as likely to stuff things into the basement where they can make me Sin-sick again. And as I go back and make amends each day, it keeps me from hurting people so much. Besides, when I go to people and make amends, I like myself better. Of course sometimes I don't do it, and sometimes I "forget" to.

When I go through my day and check these Sin-defects, I often catch myself controlling, denying, justifying my actions, and ignoring the power of God as I live in fear. And I do all these things, trying to make myself the big person who is always right and always number one. I am appalled at this, since I have honestly *felt* like a humble Christian lay witness much of the time the last few years.

Now that I can see something of the way the Disease has crippled me, I *want* to find out all I can about the ways I play God. I know that I can't serve him, help other people effectively, or experience his peace and joy unless I am in recovery from Sin. If I quit doing the things I am learning how to do to recover from the Disease, quit turning loose each day, quit meeting with other recovering people and doing the daily inventory and praying the simple prayers I pray, I know that I will slip back into my grandiose, self-centered, and frustrated life. I know this because it has happened. And now I am convinced that God's love and grace are like the manna he gave the Hebrews in the desert. They had to gather it every day. It rotted and spoiled if they tried to store it (Exod. 16: 19, 20).

So, although I can neither project what kind of a person God is uncovering in me nor "manufacture" that person through careful editing, I am finding great strength and hope—and periods of serenity—in trying to replace fear with courage one day at a time as I surrender. I am trying to "feel" my way through each day, doing the things at hand and trusting him with the outcome. And he is teaching me some new ways of seeing and being.

14

Some Learnings from Prayer

I have found release from stress and a sense of closeness to God in simply expressing my present authentic feelings to him and allowing myself to
experience them: "Lord, I hurt today." "I am lonely
this evening." "I feel sad." Or, "I am filled with joy
and peace right now, Lord. Thank you!" Sometimes
as I just *say* these feelings out loud, I begin to smile
or weep for sadness or joy as I connect with the words
I am saying to him. When I share my feelings aloud
with God I feel that I am more truly present with him.
These were unfamiliar thoughts and experiences to
me as I began to pray as a surrendering sinner.

I have met people who visualize God on a throne
in heaven, or in a chair in the room they are in. Others
have no visual image when they pray, and still others
pray only kneeling. Some pray silently, and some pray
out loud. I now think they all might be right. I believe
that whatever brings me to God's presence so that I

can surrender and ask his help to find and do his will is very likely right for me. I'm convinced that God accepts each of us as we are. Evidently, as long as we are trying sincerely to communicate with him, he will be receptive to our attempts.

A Less Compulsive Way

I decided that I was going to spend the rest of my life learning how God made me to live—believing that he really wants sanity and wholeness for me. Having made that decision I wasn't in such a big hurry (some of the time) to learn everything at once. I am beginning to believe that I really can trust him to teach me and change my life and that he will do these things just as fast as I am ready for him to.

My problem seems to be that I still resist letting God change me. My old habits are painful but familiar, and I am afraid of the unknown. Yet in spite of my fears I now am letting him change some lifelong harmful habits.

Lifelong Pattern Changes

As I write this I don't know whether or not you who are reading these words can know what it is like to be a driven person, always taking on more commitments, duties, and obligations than you can handle comfortably. I don't know if you have gone to bed, staring at the ceiling, feeling frantic about the fact that you have more to do the next day than you can possibly get done—yet unable to see how you can cancel anything because you have *agreed* to do it all. But this compulsive working/committing has been a way of life for me.

So when I tell you that I almost never work at night now, that I canceled all my traveling speaking commitments for almost two years, and that I am saying no to all kinds of things that in the past have kept me from having some peaceful time with my wife, I'm hoping you will realize what a miracle that is. I know now that, for me, saying yes too much was diseased behavior. I was so grandiose I thought I could do much more in a day than is possible for me—and I made my commitments accordingly—*for years*. Having made the commitments, I *had* to fulfill them—even if I was feeling sick or had obviously overcommitted. After all, as the "one in the center" I couldn't let people think I was only a tired, stupid human being who had made a mistake and agreed to do more than he could handle.

As my denial cracked open, I saw how I was working like crazy to justify myself and not face my self-importance and pride. When I had thought about the price I was paying to fulfill all those commitments, I'd used words to myself like "conscientious" and "integrity at great cost." Now I was seeing that the truth about me and the cause of my dilemma had more to do with "grandiosity" and "being too proud to admit I'd overscheduled."

So for me to be living a quiet, sane life, working a fairly normal number of hours a day, and doing that calmly instead of at a high-pressure, high-anxiety pace, is indeed like being born again. Often during the day I just look up, shake my head, and say, "Thank you, God."

We Are Not Talking About Sainthood Here

Sometimes I forget about my commitment to God, get panicky, and go into my old fear/anxiety syndrome. And when I do, I try to stop, confess that I am not trusting God, and surrender my whole life to him. I try to realize that if I don't get done what I'd planned, I can do it tomorrow. I can call people I've made commitments to if I need to and tell then that I've overcommitted and can't make a deadline. If I get a strong negative reaction, I will learn to call sooner or to not overcommit—since I know I can't do as much as I thought I could.

If that doesn't get me calm again, I call a fellow traveler on the road to recovery. Or I call my minister or my spiritual mentor. (Mentors and ministers are usually not surprised by such calls.) I ask him to pray for me, tell him that I'm into my old diseased thinking. He usually tells me to pray, to turn my will and my life over to God, and to go to a meeting as soon as possible with some other recovering folks. (See meetings described in Section IV.) Or he may tell me he can't talk now but he'll call me in an hour—or whenever he can.

What I am trying to describe is a way of living in which we consciously and specifically ask God and his people for help. We ask them to help us see and change those self-centered, diseased behaviors that make us miserable and hurt our relations with God and people around us.

Listening for God to Speak Through My Inner Child

I have realized that most of my life I tried to please certain people around me so much that I finally lost track of my own inner voice and didn't really know who I was or what I wanted to do with the rest of my life. Although it had not been a conscious thing, I had been a people-pleaser to get the love and affirmation I've been so hungry for.

Let's say my wife and I were going out. I might say, "What movie would you like to see?" "What would you like to eat tonight?" Even if I had a certain restaurant I wanted to go to, I'd go where she wanted in order to please her. This may have looked like unselfishness, but the truth was that I was so out of touch with my own feelings and needs that I often *didn't know* what I wanted. I'd had to stay in the center and please other people to make sure I could maneuver to get what I needed, which was their attention and approval.

And now in the relative quietness inside, I'm beginning to hear and see what my inner child is like and what he wants and needs to fulfill God's purpose in his life. He is much more shy than I would have suspected and is tired of trying to impress people with all of the work and accomplishments. And as I check what I am hearing from within myself with my mentor and my friends on this spiritual journey, they help me. They tell me they think that God is guiding me to be more honest and more true to the way he made me—which I have evidently never thought was "enough."

Time for My Body—A New Part of Being God's Person

My attitude concerning just about everything began to change. I started to realize that in making my over-sized plans for success in the future, I had "not had time" for rest and physical renewal. My wife, Andrea, wrote a book in which she pointed out that the only material tool God has given us with which to do his will is our bodies. And when we neglect to take care of our bodies we are seriously affecting our ability to serve him.[1]

I began to look at the meals I was eating and thank God for the good tastes and the fact that I could change my body by eating healthy food, getting enough rest, and engaging in a sound exercise program, which I am doing.

Giving Up Control of My Destiny—And Everyone Else's

As I've said before, when I began to concentrate on the present I was actually giving up control of my future "destiny" and of the irreparable past. If God had given me so many good things already, surely I could trust him to do it in the future. As I seemed to be giving up control of my world (which my experience had shown me I was really powerless to control anyway), God began to show me a new kind of control. I began to see that I do have quite a bit of control but only in deciding to change *me* and my *own* life.

I saw that I am not *supposed* to change the people around me—even my children. God evidently has a special adventure for each person in his world. That adventure involves failure and success, and lessons to be learned to help us develop into those persons we are to become. If I jump in and fix people up, trying to be the big helper (which I've done), I often keep them from learning the lessons they *need* to learn about how to cope in the world.

For instance, if I try to ease my children's financial burdens too much they may not take financial burdens seriously and learn how to make the choices necessary to deal with them. I have a friend who made a lot of money; he told me years later that he had made all his brothers and sisters millionaires—and "ruined their lives." It's not bad to help people, but if the motive is to "fix" them or to be the "big influence in their lives," the helping often smacks of Sin. Besides, if God is the director of everyone's adventure I really don't know what is best for the people around me. I'm judging what I think is best—as if I *were* God. Now I just try to support people near me and stand by them when they are having problems—rather than rush in and "solve" their problems before they have a chance to "listen to them" and see what God may be saying through the difficulties.

So unless I am asked (or unless there is an emergency, like an accident), I try not to give advice or fix situations—and I have taken a lot of "pride" in being "the fixer" all my life.[2]

You may not agree with what I am saying; but, for me, not having to play God has meant a great release. And my relationships seem to be less stressful. Part of my delusion has been that I can help people solve their problems best by sharing my "knowledge" and "insights." Sometimes I have helped people that way. But I now realize that my best help is when I listen and share my experience, strength, and hope but allow people to choose their actions on their own.

This sounds easy to do as I write it, but a long-distance telephone call from someone I love who is in trouble can shatter my best resolve. I begin to spout advice in my old "subtle" way before you can say, "Give it to God."

Yet there are times when I do remember who I am and who God is. And when I do, I can stand ready to support, but surrender to God the *outcome* of, even my family's struggles. And I can often let him stay up all night worrying while I go to sleep. Far from feeling guilty because I can't "fix it," I often am thanking God for what he has done for me through similar pain that has helped me to begin growing up.

This may sound callous to you, but then you may not be as gripped by the need to please people or be "The Solution" as I've been.

When I concentrate on changing my own character defects, these changes make me realize more and more how much there actually is that I need to work on.

I realize that the process I am describing is counter to the workaholic model for "success" in America (and sometimes in the church), with its demand for ever-increasing productivity. The volume of my work and the number of people I contact have *de*creased. But I am discovering instead a way to live and work in which the purpose is to enjoy living, working, and helping people as a part of loving God. The results and "volume" are his problem; mine is to make the necessary simple plans for the future and then to live fully in the present. And for me this has great meaning.

Another Kind of Turning Loose—of Words

I've always been terribly verbal. I talk things to death, often repeating an idea in several ways when it's already clear to the person I'm talking to (you may have noticed). And I've done that with God too.

But since I've seen the way the Disease uses my words to hide behind and to manipulate with, I am being less talkative in my prayers. When I pray for a sick friend or a family member, for instance, I usually just picture myself holding the person I'm praying for up to God in my cupped hands as a child, and then putting the friend in God's cupped hands in trust, saying to him, "Thy will be done."

I realize that some people I pray for are very sick. If I only pray for them to live and they do, they may live but wind up being "vegetables." I want the best for them, and I figure God does too. I assume that since healing was such a large part of the Bible story God wants sick people healed in some way, unless it is time for their life to end—which may be a greater healing experience from God's perspective. Although I'd grieve terribly for some of them, I know that death may be the loving answer to my prayer.

For years I prayed specifically about everything, feeling I was helping the doing of God's will by the things I prayed for. But I've seen that I understand very little about the specifics of God's will, or how to live. I know now that my prayers were often attempts to get God to do my will for a person or situation— as if I knew and was informing him of the "best plan." Now I know I have to *listen* to God to get a clue as to how to break through my denial and delusion and love people—including myself—for him.

I don't pray much for myself anymore. Mostly I just ask, "Please show me your will for me today." Then I sit quietly for a few minutes in a listening attitude. Next I think about what is already before me to do this day. And I get up and start doing it. I have found that doing the job at hand is the best way for me to find the next thing God may have for me.

This is not magic. And I do not often get immediate "verbal instructions." Sometimes all I get is a sense of peace and the assurance that all is well. Now I am more willing to move forward with that as the only answer until a more specific one develops within or comes from other people. But sometimes as I listen, I do realize specific things I need to do to love people and to maintain my own sanity and commitment to God. And I make notes. I usually close all my prayers by saying, "Not my will but thine be done."

I believe that the purpose of prayer is not to get things I want but, in fact, to get to know God and *his* ways of doing and being. I have learned that his ways are often very different from mine and a lot better. I have become hesitant to pray for specific things. If I believe that God loves me and all people and can in fact take better care of us than we can take of ourselves, then my job is to learn to *hear* what he is saying to me. I need to learn what kinds of things *he* has in mind for me to do and be, because I believe those things will bring me to the destiny and life that will most fulfill his designs *and* my deepest dreams and potential. *My* ideas of what would be good for me have often been warped and colored by my Sin.

An Example

For example, years ago when I first made a commitment to God as a young man I wanted to be a successful independent oil operator. I became exploration manager for an oil company when I was about thirty; then I went into a partnership with two outstanding men. We started small, but it looked to me as if my dreams were coming true. I was *telling* God that this dream was what I wanted. But I was working compulsively and wasn't listening for his signals through my body. I "denied" that I was getting ulcers and was anxious all the time when I was working. In any case, the deal our group made that was supposed to put us in a secure business position went sour. I was very disappointed, but in my discouragement I went to God in my prayer and turned my vocational future over to him.

Almost immediately a strong desire to go back and finish the theological degree I'd started years before came to me. It seemed totally right, and the man I studied with, Elton Trueblood, was the man who encouraged me to write.

Years later, as I thought about what had happened, I realized that God's will for me and the vocation he evidently had for me had been buried beneath my own dreams and prayers about being a big oil producer. Until that vision got out of the way, I couldn't hear God's dream for me. At the time that I was praying for success in the oil business, the gift of an acid stomach, no sleep, and a deal going sour hardly seemed like helpful answers to prayer. But through my feelings and my body God *was* giving me the answer I needed about his will: "This job is not right for you."

And over the years, as different things happened to me, I realized that if I had received what I had decided was God's will—what I had prayed for— often those things would have hurt me and made life quite miserable. Some of them did.

A Growing Mystery

I don't mean to be Pollyanna at all. I don't understand prayer. All I know is that the process of praying in the way I have described is changing my life and my relationships with people as well as with God. By praying specifically for men, women, or children by name but leaving the outcome in God's hands, I find that those people are on my mind and that I get insights into how I might best love them.

Recently I have begun to meditate with a pencil in

my hand, as Dr. Tournier has recommended for years. This is helping me to hear my feelings and to get in touch with silence and, I hope, with God.

As the months have gone by I am much more comfortable talking less and less to God in my prayers. I commit my life each day in simple thanksgiving, asking him to signal me through my authentic feelings, through my friends who are recovering, through the Bible, and mostly through a listening attitude as to what his will is for me. Then I ask him for the wisdom and courage to do his will today. And before I go to sleep at night I thank him for the gifts of another day.

15

Reading for "Food"

When I was a young boy, a wise older person once told me that the only doorway to the unconscious center of my heart was through my conscious mind. She said that in order to be a wise and sensitive man when I grew up I should put "wise and sensitive" things in my mind every day, and that they would seep into my heart. "One of the main ways you can 'take things in,'" she said, "is to read something enriching every day." And I believed that.

So when I surrendered to God I realized that if I wanted to change my unconscious habits and character defects that were infected by the Sin-disease it would be vital to read about God, as well as pray to him.

The Bible

The Bible is certainly not a magical book. But millions of religious people have believed that under God's supervision and guidance, his personality and purposes are expressed by, and mingled with, the lives and the history of the Hebrew people. The Bible, many millions believe, is the best place one can go to read about God. There we can discover the way God's will works out in the lives of men, women, and children as they live in the midst of the problems, joys, and pressures of the real world. We can see how he has helped people deal with the Sin-disease.

The Bible is a different kind of book than most books about religion. It assumes that God actually sticks his nose into the lives of men and women and nations and affects what happens to them. The biblical picture is that he broods over all of history—and yet "walks with us in it." Within the biblical story is the record of God's reaching out to human beings and of the human search for meaning and guidance in the committed relationship to him. It contains a running account, from beginning to end, of his people's rebellion and battle with Sin. Although we are his creatures, he seems to be trying to win us over, so that in our freedom we will choose to participate in the grand design of life that he envisions for us—and that is centered in a freely chosen and loving relationship with him. If we have committed our lives to God, the most important written information about his nature and the evolution of our new life is what we can find by immersing ourselves in the Bible.

The History of Surrender and Salvation

In the history and literature of the Hebrew people we see the struggle of the nation and the great indi-

viduals in it as they tried to learn about God and live
for him. They wrestled with the mystery of their Sin
as they ran from him, rejected him, and came back
and surrendered to him (just as we do). And they
learned that he was not just their God but the God
of the whole world. It is a fascinating story made up
of history, drama, poetry, songs, proverbs, wisdom,
literature, prophecies, parables, direct accounts of
personal experience, and some of the best narrative
writing anywhere. Through this story God is said to
have revealed himself and his purposes for the drama
of human life.

And as we surrender our lives to God and come to
his book with an open heart and mind, over the years
we can almost hear the heartbeat of God and see his
footprints along the trails the Hebrew people walked
through their history.

We can see that their ideas about God were very
primitive at first, and often crude. As the story pro-
gresses we realize that, as they developed socially, psy-
chologically, and spiritually, their ideas about
everything became more mature. And it soon becomes apparent that we can't take the early history as
being the Hebrews' final word about God. This makes
it very dangerous to quote things out of context from
the earliest history as if it is our understanding now
of the way God feels (e.g., when God is said to have
commanded that whole cities be murdered, Josh. 6–8;
or when he is said to have commanded that a man be
stoned to death for picking up sticks on the Sabbath,
Num. 15:32–36).

But paradoxically, important truths about God can
be discovered in *any* part of the Bible. I began to see

that those of us who have turned our lives over to
God are in a *cosmic* struggle against the Sin-disease,
as well as a personal struggle. The Disease has evidently infected *every living person* (Rom. 3:23), thus
every institution, with its insidious grandiosity, denial,
and delusion. I saw that Sin can be corporate and
social through the way we set up our institutions to
support our own denial and Sin. I saw that even some
of Israel's greatest spiritual leaders became so affected
by the Disease at times that they wound up being
enemies of God's love and purposes—all the while
trying to serve him (e.g., Saul, David, Solomon, and
Peter).

By the time of the New Testament the delusion and
denial of the Sadducees and Pharisees had become
monumental. Jesus' surrender to God's will, and his
accompanying rigorous honesty about the way the Sin
had permeated Israel's life, threatened to reveal to
the world the nature and depth of the Disease in their
lives and institutions. Rather than face the truth about
themselves, the leaders of Jesus' people had him
killed. And although the resurrection events are said
to have dealt a death blow to Sin and assured God's
ultimate victory, the power Jesus faced to the death
is the same power we are all dealing with *still* in our
struggles with the Sin-disease.

This is one of the paradoxes of our faith. We believe
that evil cannot win out in the end, but within history
now the battle with evil is as fierce as ever, except now
we know that if we commit our lives to God, we can
defeat the Disease—the effects of self-caused evil in
our lives—one day at a time. This need to be against
evil in God's name is a spontaneous reaction that be-

gins the moment a person contacts "the holy" in life and particularly when one meets God himself in one's own experience.

Denial and Reading the Bible

Through reading the Bible I saw that I have often thoroughly trivialized the nature of the unseen warfare with the Sin in my life, turning the struggle into a list of moral dos and don'ts and generalized ethical concerns. I blocked out the fact that the focus of the cosmic battle for *me* lies in the struggle against my own self-centered replacing of God in my life and the lives of others. My denial about this is such that I cannot remember ever being told that it says in the Bible that we are battling a terminal spiritual disease— even though I can vaguely remember concerned-looking ministers preaching that the "wages of Sin is death." I just couldn't relate *that* "Sin" to the manipulating and controlling *I* was doing of the people around me, as I continually attempted to establish my opinions and myself as "number one" among my family and associates.

My reaction to such preaching (about Sin) that I did hear was to reject those preachers who implied that *I* and people like me were sinners. I thought they were narrow-minded and were being a little fanatical. I moved on and found preachers who spoke about "love and relationships," not Sin. And when I read the Bible, I denied what I was seeing about the prophets' and Jesus' *continual* battle with the Disease. As I ask other Bible students, it seems apparent that many of us no longer even see that the struggle with the Sin-disease and with the denial of the people was perhaps the primary struggle of the prophets in the Old Testament and of Jesus and the New Testament writers.

The reaction of righteous rage in the scribes, Pharisees, and Sadducees at being called "hypocrites" and "blind guides" rang a familiar note in my experience: I was angry at people who preached about Sin. I now realize that my reaction was evidence of the operation of the same Disease and its delusion (see Matt. 15:14). Jesus described in some detail the scribes' and Pharisees' "blindness" (their denial) and told them that unless they cleaned out the inside of their lives they would remain whitewashed tombs full of rottenness and death (Matt. 23:13–28). It was quite disconcerting to realize that God was also saying that to me.

A Purpose for Life

As I have become more and more familiar with the Bible, its truth is helping me to see my own denial that my idols were success, family, control, money, sex, alcohol, good feelings, and people. And I see that I have denied and bypassed some of the hard messages in the Scriptures about taking care of the poor, not worshiping material things, and about "fame" and being a peacemaker. As I immerse myself in this story and share with other people who are trying to surrender to God, I am getting back in touch with what is real in my life and with God. I am establishing these contacts through prayer, confession and making amends, worship at church, and reexperiencing my repressed feelings and other denied reality.

And as we read the Bible thoughtfully, searching for the truth about God and ourselves, we can see that throughout the Old *and* New Testaments God was a loving God. From the beginning he wanted a new life and purpose for his people that would bring them *shalom*: peace, happiness, and health. He called them not just to "feel good" but to a glorious destiny—to lead the people in the world to "bless themselves" in spiritual wholeness and freedom from the self-defeating and blinding effect of the Sin-disease—from death itself (Gen. 22:18; Rom. 8:1, 2; John 8:51).

All That Is Necessary for Salvation Is There

Different groups of religious people have divergent views about how to look at the Bible as a document. Yet almost all agree that the guiding hand of God led those who wrote and those who selected which writing was included to make sure that all that is necessary for salvation is in the Bible. "Salvation" includes the power to face and recover from the disease we are examining. Profound pictures of wholeness, freedom, courage, and the ability to love are included in the pages of this amazing book.

Moreover, regardless of their apparent sophistication and education, or lack of these things, recovering pilgrims of all ages have discovered healing from the blindness of Sin and a way to live serenely as they have read the Scriptures. Over the years, if we read the Bible with open minds and hearts, God will teach us and guide us to deeper understandings of himself and of the hidden mysteries of our own lives.

As we read, an almost incredible thing can happen. We may discover *specific help* for problems we will face the very day we are reading. I am basically cynical about things like this, but many times I have received just the help or guidance I needed (or would need that day) as I was reading the Bible in the morning.

Reading for "Food": Devotional Reading

This sort of reading of the Scriptures, listening for truth from God for use in the practical issues of our lives, has traditionally been called "devotional" reading of the Bible. And although many times we do not feel we are "getting anything out of" the reading for a specific day, we are not to worry about that. It seems to be that over the months and years, the truths of this book will become a part of the spiritual chemistry of our lives. We unconsciously ingest the ideas and perspectives of God through Moses, Jesus, and the other actors in the story.

Without even realizing it we may begin to see the world and people more as the God of the Bible does. As we deal with our Sin and character defects and our vision clears, we may find the courage to see more and more ways in which our Disease and its denial separate us from life and from others. When we see these things, our hearts are sad or broken, and when they are we can go to our brothers and sisters who have been on the journey longer. They will give us support and help in facing our sins and changing our self-centered habits.

What long-term effects does reading the Bible devotionally have on us? At the beginning of this chapter I mentioned some advice I got as a boy to put good things into my mind each day. The woman who told me that said that in a sense people may one day become whatever truth they keep putting into their minds. I think that principle may be especially true of reading the Bible devotionally. When we read this way, we are not reading for "facts" to tell other people; we are drinking the Bible like clear water with spiritual growth vitamins in it. After a while we will find that God's Spirit will bring biblical perspectives to our conscious mind when a problem or decision comes up in our lives.

Of course, one does learn specific things, the stories of the exodus, the rise of the Hebrew kingdom, and the parables and teachings of Jesus, for instance. But I believe that the real and lasting value of devotional Bible reading is what it does for us over the long haul. As we think about the scenes and words and parables we are reading and let our imaginations put us back into the settings where the stories were taking place, we can use the Bible as an antique but accurate mirror in which we can get a glimpse behind our denial and discover the hidden character defects (and creative abilities) the Disease has caused us to stuff out of sight in our fear.

There's No Hurry in This "Race"

If we are planning to live the rest of our lives trying to learn and do God's will one day at a time, we do not need to have the sense of urgency to "learn it all today" that we Americans are so prone to. If you are trying to surrender your life and will spend a few minutes a day actually changing your behavior by planning for and keeping to a period of prayer and reading the Bible, I can almost promise you that you will be a different person in a few years—or a few months.

Since there is no hurry, one can start in one's prayer time by reading for four or five or ten minutes a day in a certain book in the Bible. I started with the Gospel of John; other people have started with Exodus, or Acts. Years ago I began by reading the Gospel of John for four or five minutes each morning. I'd then take about ten minutes to pray. Recently I heard a man who's been reading the Bible regularly for many years say that for him Bible reading had gone through three stages. At first it was like castor oil, then like shredded wheat, and finally like ice cream. I can't say that's been my experience, but the Bible has become a fascinating library (though sometimes I do need a rest from reading it).

By reading five minutes in the Gospel of John when I started, I began to become familiar with the way the Bible sounds. I didn't try to "learn a lot" but rather to see and feel what the story was lik As time went on I developed a real curiosity about the history and geography of the biblical world. I started looking at a Bible atlas and Bible commentaries.

But when I got into these kinds of books *about* the Bible, I found that I could not listen attentively to God at the same time. I would unconsciously switch from a right-brain "loving and listening person" to a left-brain "analyzing student." I realized that I needed to separate my study times from my devotional times if I was going to let God speak to my mind as well as my heart through his book. I realize that God may speak anytime one is reading the Bible. But when I have only read the Bible with an analyzing attitude or in preparing lessons to teach, I have missed the wonder of having the immediate and personal guidance of God through its pages each day. I stayed in this intellectualizing trap for several years.

I realized that I needed to spend some additional *but separate* time reading the Bible and other books in a different way. I needed a study time as well as a devotional time.

16

Reading for Understanding and Broader Vision

"**S**tudying" the Bible is a much more left-brain, logical, analytical kind of enterprise than devotional reading and is usually done with various kinds of resource books. There are Bible dictionaries in which to look up biblical words that are unfamiliar. There are Bible atlases that explain and illustrate with maps the political and geographical changes in the development of peoples and nations in the history of the Israelites. There are concordances in which one can find any word in the Bible and discover where it is used every time, so that if you know one word of a quotation you can look up that word and find the quotation you want very quickly. There are all kinds of Bible commentaries to help you understand the meaning of the Scriptures in context. All these helps and others can be used to study the Bible and to discover not only the meaning of the words and stories but what was happening in the context of the people's lives and the larger world around them as the various books and stories in the Bible were written. This sort of information can be helpful in fighting the Sin-disease in the social and political aspects of one's life as well as the personal.

Some people only read the Bible devotionally. But I think if one is seriously trying to turn one's whole life over to God, it is important to also take the time to *study* the Bible. For some people studying alone is difficult; they may find it helpful to study the Bible with a group.

Other Books About Living for God

From the beginning, I looked for reading material that would help me live as a surrendered Christian in all areas of my life. I had difficulty finding any books in which the author seemed to have the same problems I did.

After my first attempt to commit my life to God years ago on a roadside in Texas, I seemed to have doubts and recurring difficulties in almost every area of living. I tried hard to change the selfish habits I could see and live a "loving and unselfish life." I looked for books to read that talked about how to face these basic problems and how to change my behavior so that God could help me overcome them.[1]

Some of the books I discovered in those early years that were helpful to me are Sam Shoemaker's *How to*

Become a Christian, C. S. Lewis's *Mere Christianity*, and Bruce Larson's *Dare to Live Now*. I also discovered devotional classics that told how the great Christians of the ages had wrestled with some of the same problems I was facing inside my own mind as I walked the streets of the twentieth century. Some of these were Thomas à Kempis's *The Imitation of Christ*, Thomas Kelly's *A Testament of Devotion*, Pascal's *Pensées*, William Law's *A Serious Call to Devout and Holy Life*, Augustine's *Confessions*, Oswald Chambers's *My Utmost for His Highest*, Hannah Whitehall Smith's *The Christian's Secret of a Happy Life*, Scupoli's *The Unseen Warfare*, and the "anonymous" books—*One Day at a Time* and *Alcoholics Anonymous*. (Although it is focused on the particular manifestation of the Disease that is called alcoholism, this last book is *excellent* on denial and living for God one day at a time.)

I tried to read books by people who were also trying to live for God. I searched a lot, because I've always felt lonely and uncertain about which of the things I thought God was telling me to do were from God and which were simply projections of my own egotistical needs. I'm still never sure about that—especially since getting a look at my denial. But it is really helpful in seeking guidance in this matter to find other people to "listen to" through books and in person, people who seem to understand what really goes on when one tries to surrender one's life to God. Studying books like those I've listed in a group and discussing the real problems involved in fighting the Disease have been very helpful to me.

Although there are hundreds of helpful books, some of my other special contemporary companions along the way (through their writing) have been Paul Tournier, Richard Foster, Elton Trueblood, Bob Rains, Robert Johnson, Fredrick Buechner, Scott Peck, and John Powell.

A Place to Read and Grow

The way I read books like those just listed is to set aside a specific amount of time each day (which has ranged from fifteen minutes to an hour at different times in my life over the past twenty-nine years). I sit down in a comfortable place (for me it helps to read in the same place every morning when I am not traveling) with a stack of three-by-five cards and a pen. I read a few paragraphs and then think about what the author is saying. When I run across an idea that rings a bell with regard to my own struggles or joys and that I think might be helpful to me or to other people, I copy the quotation on a card along with the book title, page number, and author. I title the card according to what part of the recovering life the quote is about. (I file all these cards in file boxes by number according to where the problem comes up in the life of a person seeking God. For example, something about "turning loose" would be in an early numbered file, and something about facing death would be filed near the end of the files, etc. This is so I can find the notes later.)

The main thing I was doing in my reading was to get inside the lives of others, those writers who had tried to surrender to God. I wanted to see how they thought and how they felt as they faced and solved the problems they met in trying to be his people in the world. More recently I have looked to see how they fought the unseen warfare with the Disease.

Along with the Bible I read dozens of these spiritual biographies, devotional classics, and other kinds of books by those who were reputed to have lived for God with loving integrity and power. As I read these a few minutes each day, I was hoping that somehow I would digest the truth they had found and God would get it into my very flesh and bones. Although I feel like a rank beginner as I write these words—in that it has been only fairly recently that I have discovered my denial and delusion—I know that reading these books has kept me on the search and given me hope that I can keep coming back to God when I fail (or when I "put him on vacation" for a period of days or even weeks at a time).

Theology and Other Areas of Study

The reading and praying we have been discussing is, in fact, one nontechnical way of "doing" theology.[2] You may also want to study the specific doctrines of the religious body you affiliate with, however, or even the historical development of the basic biblical doctrines. The differences in the approaches taken by different "biblical" bodies to the study of theology are often considerable. Although you may not think these differences are important, I would suggest that you start with your own minister, rabbi, or mentor as a guide for your study of theology.

I have also found it beneficial to read something

about the philosophy of religion. And I enjoy reading novels and listening to music. It seems to me that we are in the business of discovering how God operates in all of life, so I find all kinds of reading and other forms of communication can be helpful in understanding the surrendering life and the people to whom God sent it—all of us.

A Different Attitude

I study theology very much as I would study any other body of knowledge—with one important difference: I find it helpful to begin a reading session by asking God to enter my mind and teach me what will be helpful for me to know about theology in order to better love him and to love his people.[3] I do this for two reasons: first, because I believe God's Spirit is the real teacher in the life of a person who wants to commit each day to him (see John 14:26), and second, because I think people who learn theology for other reasons (ultimately) than to help them love people and God and live for him may wind up "gaining nothing" and could set the cause of recovery from Sin back a great deal (see 1 Cor. 13:2–3).

When one studies something as an object, one classifies, judges, and criticizes. The one studying is always in control and winds up evaluating the material studied by comparing it to similar material. But the biblical message is a different kind of subject.

The essence of the Bible has to do with an *offer* by God of his love, forgiveness and guidance and of the power to defeat the Sin-disease and do his will. We can either accept or reject this offer as the hypothesis by which we will try to live our entire lives. Although I believe that we must use all our critical and analytical faculties, the danger I see is that theologians can use their critical and analytical training as a defense against God's real theological question, voiced by both Moses and Jesus, "Will you follow me? Will you surrender to me?" For most of my life my best evaluative thinking *kept me from* facing my denial and from swallowing my pride enough to admit my powerlessness to straighten my life out alone. For a long time my "best thinking" kept me from that surrender that leads to peace and joy.

Historically, the Disease seems to delight in theological study and arguments that do not lead to a more loving, recovering community. I am convinced that if one learns all there is to know about the Bible and "theology" and has not said yes and surrendered to God, then one may have dug up the whole theological field and never found the pearl that was buried in it, and the Sin-disease may be untouched in that person's life.

To help us avoid this intellectualization, our age-old defense against intimacy with him (and each other), God has given us a cleansing doorway into recovery and closeness: confession.

17

Confession: Key to Recovery—and to Worship

We are now facing the two most difficult issues about recovery from the Sin-disease for many people.

Recognizing and *admitting* that the blinding denial one has seen in the lives of others *is* also going on in one's own life.

Finding a way to *clear out* the denied, hidden debris of the past that is charged with powerful repressed feelings.

First we must discover a way to focus a clear light into the dark and shadowy regions of our lives where we have buried specific sins and character defects and hidden them even from ourselves. These buried things from our past make us very touchy. They operate like mines in an uncharted mine field protecting the citadel of our Sin. These buried sin-mines explode in fear and anger when someone innocently steps on one of them. We need to *see* and *own* these hidden sins and character defects so that we can bring them out and surrender them to God in confession. Then, as he takes them and forgives us, the feeling of "danger" evaporates for us and the people around us. We can then receive from him peace to replace the fear of someone uncovering a part of our lives and blowing up a relationship. He frees us from the struggle to look adequate and in control because we no longer have to keep our Sin and sins hidden from the world.

Resolving the first issue—recognizing and owning our denial—is made possible through our admission of powerlessness to overcome our Sin alone and the surrender of our lives and wills to God (as we understand him at that point). When we do these things the wall of denial, suddenly or gradually, cracks open and allows us to begin to *see* our self-centeredness and some of its effects on others.

The second—finding a way to shine a clear light into the shadowy corners of our lives so that we can let God clean them out—is very important. These undealt-with sins and resentments and the repressed feelings attached to them are a glut of Sin material that constipates one's spiritual life and makes the experience of living fearful and erratic. We must avoid at all cost certain areas (like "conflict" or "intimacy," depending on the person) since our feelings can explode unexpectedly when someone touches, either purposely or unwittingly, a hidden tender spot.

Turning on the Light

There is a real paradox in this process. At one level we are learning not to worry about the past, yet here we are digging it up. But as someone pointed out to me recently, this paradox has been at the center of the teaching of most great spiritual teachers. Jesus, for instance, said not to worry about money (see Matt. 6:25–31), but he also said *to* worry about other things. He said specifically to worry about "the beam in your own eye," and that's what we are beginning to deal with through a specific confession.

After turning our wills and lives over to God, the first step to freedom from the mine field of repressed sins is through the doorway of the specific confession of what we *can* see of our past.

As a person in recovery begins to perceive how he or she has hurt people, the natural response is to feel sadness and/or guilt about what he or she has done. The sadness produces the motivation to turn away from the sin and confess it to God, asking for his power and help not to repeat the harmful behavior.[1]

A person not only confesses the act of putting him- or herself in the center where only God belongs but also makes explicit (in detail) as many of the shadowy deeds and thoughts as he or she can see at that time. Compulsions and addictions are faced along with the accompanying harmful behaviors.[2] This act of confession brings these hidden sins out of the memory and can expel them and their destructive power from the heart.

Once a person has confessed to God all the specific

sinful acts he or she can recall, the past is clean. One is forgiven and can embrace the gift of a new chance at life. It is as if God had erased the blackboard on which the sins had been listed in the confessing person's mind, and handed over a piece of chalk and said, "Here, you can write a new chapter for your life." The peace, joy, and motivation to live for God that come from these actions is incredible: one's spiritual life can come alive!

In addition to the gift of a new life, God gives the confessed the security of his love and forgiveness. The one who has been forgiven no longer needs to hide his or her Sin from God. The forgiven person can then afford to see even farther behind the walls of delusion and denial and begin to have a clearer and deeper view of the harmful behaviors and attitudes that have been brought on by Sin.

Thus the confessing person begins breaking the deadly and exhausting cycle of hiding behind compulsions and addictions and enters a cleansing process of confession and forgiveness that is life-renewing and energizing. The confession process leads to serenity, joy, and freedom from (1) guilt from the past, (2) the Sin-disease and its accompanying compulsions and addictions in the present, and (3) fear of the Disease's slippery slide toward death in the future.

Facing Our Hidden Past

But how do we *do* this specific housecleaning today when everyone seems to be embarrassed by the idea of confession and horrified at the prospect of revealing anything that might make them look inadequate or sinful?

The saints have given us an answer to this dilemma regarding the exhuming of our buried sins, but this course of action is so terrifying that many of us in contemporary religious denominations have discarded it as too severe a remedy. This is one way it works: we begin cleaning out the debris of the past by making a thorough examination of our own lives and bringing what we find out into the light (see 1 John 1:5–9).

We are to face our character defects and moral transgressions with all the thoroughness we can put together and with rigorous honesty. But we are also to include in our inventory the *positive* character traits and abilities that God has given us. These are the assets through which he will work to fight the Disease.

In my case, before I could begin a serious journey into the radical changes that would follow the daily disciplines of living a new life, I needed to clear my path of the pitfalls and snarling vines growing out of the past, and also to inventory the assets and gifts I had with which to fight the Disease.

I needed to see clearly what was in my life so the Disease would have nothing mysterious to hide behind or scare me with; because by this time I knew that my Sin would use anything that "pushes my buttons" to threaten me with: the specter of failure, fears, guilt, rejection, and spiritual death.

For me it was crucial to make as clean a beginning as possible if I hoped to stay close to God.

Transferring Assets and Liabilities

When we commit our lives to God, I was told, it's as if we are agreeing to transfer to him all the assets and liabilities of a business we own. If we were doing that we would take an inventory of the damaged goods and the valuable assets that are stored in the warehouse of the past. And to give God these things, we must make the inventory very *specific*.

We must *face* and *name* the actions, character traits, resentments, fears, sins, and positive abilities we have stored in our basements. Since God already knows what is in us, the real purpose of the inventory is to help *us* to get in touch with those things that are blocking us (and those sins and abilities we have denied) so that we can offer them to God and let him forgive us and use the inventory as a guide for the program of living he will design for us.

For example, I have certain resentments that have crippled and captured my life. As I list these resentments and face them, he can show me what it is that caused me to be resentful. He can show me (and has) patterns in the way I set myself up to be resentful—which I've discovered I do.

For instance, for years I would, on occasion, do something helpful for someone that might cost a significant amount of money or time. I would tell myself (and sometimes the "helpee") that I didn't expect anything in return. But if the person I'd helped did not express what I considered to be "reasonable" gratitude, I resented him or her—a lot. I saw that my dishonesty about my expectations set me up to resent people I wanted to help.

I saw that I also resented anyone who threatened to reveal my Sin, my controlling self-centeredness, or threatened the symbols of my adequacy (e.g., my reputation, my material possessions, or my sex life). For example, whenever anyone confronted me about trying to control a situation or a person, I was embarrassed and resentful, even if the accusations were true—perhaps especially if they were true. I also resented people who were outstanding in my field who didn't agree with my approach or who gossiped about me (or whom I perceived as gossiping about me), as well as men who flirted with my wife in ways that made me think they wanted her sexually. When I first began this examination I didn't think I resented anyone. I was in denial about that too.

But when I began seeing and confessing the resentments I *could* perceive, then I could see that my pride and possessiveness had set me up to be resentful. I saw that as I confessed my pride and possessiveness, I was less likely to be trapped and miserable when someone threatened to reveal them. I could sometimes change my controlling attitude about people and things in my life and not set myself up to be resentful again and again, as I've done in the past.

And it's not just people I have resented. There are institutions and ways of thinking and acting that are not like mine. I resented actions (or inaction) of the church, the Russians, the United States (domestic and foreign policy), the IRS.

I saw that as long as I have resentments about other people, those people control me in a real way. I am forced to think about them and what they have done to me. As one friend said, I am letting such people "live rent-free in my head." Besides, resentments emit a poison that kills peace and joy on contact. I realized that if I want to survive and grow in my spiritual life I must learn how to give up my resentments.

What could I do? I knew by this time that I was powerless to quit resenting someone on my own. But my recovering friends told me that it had helped them to realize that to some degree everyone out there is sick (as we are sick) with the Sin-disease. Many of them are still in denial and can't even see the effect of their behavior on others. Some couldn't care less. So I tried to think of those people I resented as being trapped, sick with the Disease as I am.

When I began to see the additional character defects and sins I had denied, I felt a lot of shame and guilt, and this increased my feelings of unworthiness. But the Bible and my recovering friends told me that when God made me, he made me a precious child of value who has some good qualities to build on—just as he did everyone else. I heard someone also on this journey say that the feelings of insecurity I was having were normal for people in the process of learning how to face themselves and live for God. The acceptance and lack of critical judgment I was discovering in a group of people who had heard me share accounts of some of my "unacceptable" behavior made me feel safer and less defensive as I examined my life.

I was told to find also the *positive* things about myself, so I could start to claim these traits and cultivate them to counteract the feelings of worthlessness that might come to me as I started to face the "negative" parts of my life.

Write It Down

The first step I found valuable in making this inventory was to get out a pencil and paper and begin to list on paper everyone whom I resented or with whom I have been angry. After each name I put what it was that I felt led to my being angry. But the issue here is not what other people have done to me but my *own* behavior and reactions. So I wrote down *my* resentments, anger, fear, and jealousy about what happened. I realize now that I can't change anyone else, but I see that I can find wholeness and serenity by dealing with my *own* feelings and behavior.

Next I listed the people I know that I have hurt, and specifically what it was I did that hurt them. And I included my own name on the list, since I have probably hurt myself more than anyone else has.

Character Defects

Next, with all the honesty I could muster I listed those character defects that I'm aware of, like lying, intense selfishness, gossiping, putting down other people to make myself look better, always having to be right, defending against the unflattering truth about myself by making alibis or justifying myself, trying to manipulate and control the lives of the people around me and instruct them about what they ought to do and be, buttering people up or complimenting them in order to get them to like me or think that I'm smart, or showing off or bragging in subtle ways to try to overcome my own sense of not being very much. It was very difficult for me to face the fact that I do these things. I have denied them to myself for years— and yet I can remember having had glimpses of each one at times. And as I wrote them down, the fog of my denial lifted and I saw them starkly.

Finding the Good News About Me Too

When I had finished listing my resentments and character defects, I began to write the good qualities about my life. This was also very difficult, since I had denied some of these too, having been taught not to claim goodness or positive traits because it would seem like bragging. But I forced myself to list the good qualities I could see about myself, like the fact that I do care about people and that I am a conscientious person and a hard worker. I wrote down things like the fact that I want very much to be honest, that sometimes I act courageously in spite of my fears, and that I do love my family and have provided for them.

As I was doing all these things I was told that I was beginning an attack on the Disease by making specific changes in my behavior. "If you try to argue one on one with the Disease," they told me, "it will win in the long haul. And if you change only your philosophy about addictions and your ideas about God, you will wind up right back where you were before long—in the clutches of the Disease. But when you are honest about and change your behavior in certain ways, beginning with making a thorough inventory, you are building a new life that is not based on your Disease. And God can give you a new kind of strength to overcome its power—one day at a time." I was finding that my friends in recovery were right.

But after having written this inventory of the negative and positive aspects of my life, I still didn't feel *rid* of the bad things or able to concentrate on the good ones. I saw that I had more work to do before I could be freed from the powerful patterns I was uncovering.

Tell It All to Another Trusted Human Being

The next step that I am about to recommend may not be for everyone, but it meant a great deal in moving me out of the land of "the-fear-of-being-known-and-rejected" and into a place where serenity and happiness are commonplace.

Many people who have longed for the freedom and serenity of God have taken the list in hand. Here on paper are the harmful, deadly, and self-defeating sins, character traits, and resentments of which we are aware, and the positive character traits that we can remember.

When you are at this point, I was advised, seek out another surrendering person whom you trust and share that list. It's not that God needs to know our self-centered character traits and harmful behaviors: he already does. But *we* need to clear out the basement of our lives from the past by bringing these things out in the open. We need the humility that the experience brings in order to clear our *vision* so we can see God's light in the denied corners of our lives.

The biblical message is that God is light, that he only lives in light. And until we walk with our lives in the light of his truth, we walk in darkness and are not cleansed. (See again John 1:5–9). To walk in the light is to live in the presence of God and to know one's own character as it truly *is* in the judgment of God. "As light is 'reality,' to walk in the light means to live in the reality of moral truth about one's self—thus to walk in the light requires rigorous honesty with God and the acknowledgement and confession of sin."[3]

Choose the Person You Tell Carefully

Choose the person you are going to read your lists to carefully! This is a difficult thing to do, but it is not as impossible as it sounds at first—particularly if you find a person who has already taken this step.

The person you choose to read your inventory list to may be your minister or a trusted friend. He or she (someone of the same sex preferably) may be a psychologist or a minister you do not know personally (Episcopal and Roman Catholic priests are often accustomed to such requests), or you may choose a member of Al-Anon or the Adult Children of Alcoholics (or another Twelve-Step program) who has taken this step. You are not looking for advice but only for a person with a nonjudgmental listening ear who will not be hurt by your confession.

My experience, and that of thousands of others, is

that we had to get our specific sins and character defects, as well as our gifts and abilities, out of the isolation of our inner life.

For years as a committed Christian I had tried to clean up my life without this step. I was like a man who kept fumigating his house but had a basement full of dead dogs. Things sometimes looked clean to me—but they never "smelled" quite right. For me it was necessary to humble myself by reading my inventory before God and another person. As I told my secrets, they lost some of their power over me, and I wasn't so afraid to be known. It was only then, through the sense of God's forgiveness that followed, that I became able to make amends, where feasible, and to find the serenity and joy of living in the light, as the biblical writers speak of it. The relief was enormous.

This process of confession and forgiveness will evidently continue the rest of our lives. And the church has recognized this in structuring its liturgy for worship.

18

Corporate Worship and "Garbage Disposal"

For years corporate worship was not an important aspect of my faith—although I attended Sunday services regularly. Often I found myself bored with the liturgy. But the last few years, and especially since I have begun to face my Sin, I have found corporate worship to be a real and necessary help in my recovery from the Disease.

I now see it as a source and sign of the recovering community—a lifeline of hope and celebration for "Diseased humanity." For years worship was a hard thing for me to talk about. My own experience with liturgies was not very positive; I was eager to get to the sermon, which I hoped would deal rationally with the difficulties I was having in trying to live for God.

I couldn't yet see that the music, the candles, the reading in unison, along with the stained glass windows and the movement through the liturgy, were all ways to get beneath our intellectual defenses and denial into the intuitive and emotional center where the Disease wrestles for control of our lives. Ministers kept telling me that worship was the "most important thing" for a believer, so I felt guilty about being bored—but I was. The focus of my own worship was the private prayer time I had developed at home and the praying I did with the small groups I attended.

But the Garbage Keeps Accumulating

Almost immediately I realized that being surrendered to God was not an easy state to maintain. I kept taking over the control of my life and "storing" my faith up in my head while unconsciously in my gut I worked and manipulated people and things trying to handle the everyday emergencies caused by the fear and anger in my life. Because of my denial I often didn't *know* I wasn't depending on God. All I knew was that sometimes things didn't seem to be going well with my faith. And often I wasn't happy.

God as Garbage Collector

About that time I remembered what a friend had told me years ago: that corporate worship (at least for Christians) was in one sense an occasion for spiritual "garbage disposal" as well as a celebration time.

At first I was a little horrified at the term *garbage disposal*, but then I saw that there was a valuable truth in what he was saying. I knew I came to worship with my gratitude *and* my garbage. But I could only remember being encouraged to contribute my gratitude and my tithe in the service; I would trudge home with my garbage still hidden in the closets and basement of my life. Consequently worship services didn't have much authentic joy for me.

But my mature friend had told me that confession in worship was a weekly dumping of our sins and failures, our spiritual garbage, into God's hands—and that he wants to collect it and take it out of our lives.

In a sense the regular confession and forgiveness transaction in worship clears the windows and opens the doors of my life to let God and other people in again. When I dump my garbage regularly in worship through confession and receive God's forgiveness, *then* I feel enormous relief and release. Praise and gratitude are spontaneous and natural responses for me as I sing and thank God in the corporate hymns and prayers. Without confession and forgiveness there was for me little joy and enthusiasm in the praising and singing parts of the service.

After I *hear* sermons and Scripture readings and confess, I am not blocked by and obsessed with my own failure and Sin. I am more likely to be interested in how I am to find and do God's will each week after he has picked up my garbage and left me a clean place in which to live and work.

Progress—Not Perfection

As time went on I saw that my perfectionism was a big part of the Sin-disease in my life. The Disease kept telling me that I should "always do it right"—whatever "it" was. So I had tried to do and say everything perfectly—even confession. But since I never could be perfect, I was constantly setting myself up for failure and guilt or denial. Now I realize that I am just supposed to do the best I can each day and bring any failures to God in worship. Through his Spirit he will take all my garbage—my failures and sins—and make it into a spiritual fertilizer for my future growth toward wisdom, understanding, and compassion.

Private Confession as Preparation for Worship

Some churches provide for private confession, individual absolution, and a sacramental statement of God's forgiveness. This is often done on Saturday prior to Communion on Sunday. I used to think private confession was spooky—until I tried it. It helped me at a crucial time in my life when I was unable to forgive myself. When the minister, in the name of the whole church, told me personally that God had forgiven me, I was freed in a deeper way. I knew that God could do the job by himself, but a time came when I needed the grace and power that came through the personal experience with that Episcopal minister.

A lot of people go to their own ministers or another

minister for the sacrament of confession regularly.

Weekly confession is simply taking an inventory of one's life since the last confession and reading it or telling it to the minister privately. In the name of the church the minister pronounces the forgiveness God offers to us all.[1]

But the focus of worship is not on our sins; it is on God and our gratitude to him.

19

Worship: Baptism, Communion, and Preaching

The worship practices of different biblical traditions vary enormously. In this chapter I am witnessing to what worship in the Christian tradition to which I belong means to me.

When I started to look at worship as something that could be specifically real and helpful to me in fighting Sin, I began to have a new appreciation for the two specific sacraments or corporate services most churches share. A *sacrament* as I am using the term means an outward and visible sign of an inward and spiritual grace (free gift from God).

These two sacraments, baptism and Communion, give us outward ways to express publicly our gratitude to God and our commitment to deal with the Sin-disease. They help us with our surrendering and in dealing with the recurring character defects that continue to plague us after we decide to commit our lives to him. And they can give us much more as they free us and send us back out into the world to do God's will.

Baptism

The first sacrament is baptism. When we want to turn from our past and turn toward God through surrender, the church has often used the phrase "dying to our old life and being reborn into a new life" to describe what happens. As we recognize our powerlessness without God to battle Sin successfully, we come before the church and announce publicly in baptism that we are joining God in the battle. We are recentering our lives in God and his will. By turning our lives over to God, we gain the gift of a new access to God's power. To help people experience and express this transition the church uses the sacrament of baptism, which is like a doorway into the family of God, a sacramental doorway we go through alone—in the midst of the fellowship—to claim God's power and accept his love.

A young woman, for example, who wants to be baptized, first makes a private statement of intention to give her entire life to God, then puts herself in the hands of the minister, who is standing in a body of water. The minister lowers the initiate's body completely under the water. This symbolizes the surrender to God and the intentional death and burial of the old life she has turned from. The minister says that he or she is baptizing the convert in the name of God (Father, Son, and Holy Spirit). When the initiate is brought up out of the water, it is symbolic of coming out of the grave (in which the old life has been buried) and being "born again" into a new life of seeking God's will. When experienced in this way baptism can bring strong feelings of joy and peace.

Several years ago I was immersed in the Jordan River by my friend Bruce Larson, as I renewed my baptismal vows. I remember the stark realization as I went under water that I was actually intending to change my whole life from then on with God's help. The physical sensation of going under water and coming out new was very emotional to me. The act of trusting God and another human being as I was immersed on my back in that cold river changed something inside me in a way I can't explain. And these things done in the presence of a group of committed believers helped make my intention to be God's person concrete and specific in a new way.

Because of the lack of available bodies of water in some places where the early Christians went, the church began to recognize the pouring or sprinkling of water on the new convert as a valid substitute for being totally immersed in baptism—if the symbolic importance of the dying and being reborn aspects of the act were explained. But however it is done, the importance of baptism as a doorway, a birth, into God's family has remained in almost all Christian bodies.

I feel sad when I realize that some churches have become bored with the service of baptism, or felt that it takes too much time, and have moved it out of the corporate worship of the people into a private corner. Baptism done in the midst of the congregation's worship allows all Christians present to review and renew their own commitment and relationship with God as they say the words of commitment with the new member they are welcoming into God's family.

The feelings of the person coming into the church—and those of the other family members— are often feelings of joy in being accepted and welcomed into the larger family by those other worshipers present. The convert is the center of the loving attention of the entire church. I believe that this is important for everyone concerned—even if the person being baptized is very young.

Holy Communion

There is a second special sacramental act of worship that is called Holy Communion or Eucharist (Eucharist means "thanksgiving"). Other churches call this service Communion or the Lord's Supper. This is a central act of worship that we in the church believe Jesus instituted the night before his crucifixion. He told us to "do this in remembrance of me" (see Luke 22:19). The meaning of this service—and "what really happens" to the people who participate in it with open minds and hearts—varies a great deal from one Christian denomination to another. But all seem to believe that the Lord meant for this service to be special.

In the Communion service we can express and affirm several almost inexpressible things. As we enter the service, it's like a new "turning loose" and trusting ourselves into the flow of God's love and care. Or it's like an earthly taste of the heavenly banquet with God and those who have gone before. There is a pervading sense of receiving fellowship, joy, and renewed power and encouragement from God and each other.

For those of us who are trying to turn our lives over to God each day and who realize how often we fail in our battles with the Disease, the Communion service can offer a unique way to deal with our failure and to gain new motivation and strength to do God's will.

The Communion liturgy tells God's story of the gift of himself through the life, death, and resurrection of Jesus (to save us from Sin) every time we participate in the service. Then, when each of us comes with our sack of failures and sins, the spiritual "garbage" I mentioned earlier, or with our grief or pain, or with sins in our past of which we are becoming aware, he gives us a place to lay these things in his hands and be cleansed as he sends us out with a new start each week.

When I come to Communion with my sack of Sin-garbage on my back, I imagine that the communion rail is a moving conveyor belt that goes directly to God. I heave the sack of confessed sins off my back, put it on the conveyor belt, and send all my pain and failure up to him. I feel as if he thanks me for trusting him with the unacceptable reality of my life, and feel that he washes me in a silver light as I kneel there, so that I can start the week clean and new inside. For me this is a very real part of the miracle of his forgiving love.

Then, when I receive the bread and wine, symbolizing the taking of the life and spirit, the body and blood of God himself, into my life, I imagine that his actual healing and strengthening life and spirit are coming into my body. I imagine these things going to the farthest corners of my personality—conscious and unconscious—through my bloodstream, as I digest the simple elements, and I am ready to go back into the world.

The cleansed feeling and the sense of power and presence that can come through the experience of Holy Communion have become a constantly renewing fountain of joy and gratitude for me when I really want to give up control in my life to God and be made serene and new.

Preaching

For many Christians preaching is the most important thing about corporate worship. Before I began to see my denial, preaching was not "relevant" to me if it dealt with denied issues that needed changing in *my* life. When the preacher talked about those who were grandiose and "playing God in other people's lives," I cheered. After all, *I* was against those things too. (I have since learned that when I find something especially distasteful in another person's behavior, that very thing is almost surely a character trait of my own that I am in denial about. In fact, my mentor told me that one way to see what I am denying is to make a list of things that especially irritate me about those around me—and then put my name at the top of the page. "These," he said, "will be a pretty accurate picture of what you are denying about *yourself*." An incredible experience—and although I would not have believed it, for me in some way, each item was true.)

Now that I am surrendering each day, I *want* to know how to face the unreality in my life. Even if it's painful, I want to discover my harmful and self-defeating behaviors and change my life, so I can serve God and live with serenity. Now I try to listen very carefully to the sermon when I find myself either getting angry *or* agreeing with the minister about certain sins "other people" need to face. Now, unless I realize the message is about me, I feel especially embarrassed when I wish some friend or family member "were present to hear this sermon."

"Biblical" Preaching

The Bible is a uniquely effective book for helping those of us who have seen our powerlessness to defeat Sin on our own. On almost every page are affirmations about the God and the "family" into whose hands we have abandoned ourselves.

In vivid color God is shown (among other things) to be

Powerful (enough to defeat Sin and even death)
Loving (enough to die for us)
Forgiving (enough so that the number of times we sin is not the point)
Righteous (enough that he will not let us off the hook

when we try to get into denial and ease back
into our diseased behavior)

Omnipresent (enough that he is with each of us always)

Omniscient or all-knowing (enough that none of our
Sins, failures, or troubled lives or relationships
is too complex for him to understand)

Sensitive to our needs (enough that he even takes care
of the birds and flowers; we don't need to be
anxious about anything in today or tomorrow
as we seek his kingdom and righteousness)

These and many more of God's always-present
characteristics are revealed in the Bible. Biblical
preaching helps us know how to live in relation to
God as well as people. But it also aids us in getting to
know and remember the great things God is, and has
to bring us, as we attempt to find and do his will.

I would like to know more about what the Word
of God has to say concerning the symptoms of and
recovery from the Sin-disease. Fortunately, the Bible
is filled with stories of how God helps his people
face their Sin and return to him—again and again,
as *we* have to do—so regular biblical preaching is
especially important for a recovering sinner. Preaching that is not based on the Bible often does not
seem relevant to a Christian who is trying to confront
the Disease.

The miracle is that when a sensitive minister is
preaching from the Scriptures, God often has a way
of bringing truth that the newly surrendered person
needs through whatever sermon is preached.

Don't Blame Things on the Church or Minister, But Find What You Need to Survive

Until I was confronted with my Sin, I kept blaming things on the church I attended or a particular minister. Now I can see that *I* am responsible for my own problems and my own recovery as a child of God. But I also see clearly that what I am describing as "confronting the Sin-disease" is not a popular way to live in many churches. We sometimes have bruised, lonely institutions in denial because we are a bruised, lonely people in denial. Because of God's love and the support we receive from his people, however, we can confess our powerlessness and begin again through our corporate worship and life together to do battle with the Disease that so often has stifled our lives and our worship.

John Calvin defined the church as existing where the Word is preached and the sacraments administered. Most Christian bodies would meet these criteria. After years of trying to find and do God's will, for me the sacraments and biblical preaching are basic necessities for survival and growth while confronting the Disease.

I am grateful for the church to which I belong. Our minister preaches biblical sermons, and I'm glad I have learned to appreciate the liturgy, especially as it is manifested in baptism and the Eucharist. These sacraments have become the most meaningful parts of my own experience of our church's life and corporate worship.

For me the bottom line about worship is that a recovering person can't make it alone. The type of corporate worship that helps me learn how to love God and praise him, and to confront my Sin effectively, is very important.

But besides corporate worship I've found that I can't make it without a certain kind of regular giving and receiving from individuals in small groups.

IV

A New Look at "Two or Three Gathered Together ..."

20

The Necessity of Sharing the Adventure: Meeting Together

For a proud, insecure person who hates to look inadequate, the idea of asking other people for help about my personal life was bad news. But everyone I respected who had tried seriously to live a surrendering life *alone* said the lone ranger stance was impossible.

"The Disease always wins," they said. And the serious Bible student will find little to justify the solo approach. But I have always been such a loner that I kept hoping I could live without all the trouble, time, and vulnerability of meeting on a regular basis with other people who were trying to recover from Sin. So I tended to redouble my personal spiritual disciplines and tried to orchestrate my own answers to life's most painful personal and relational problems.

But the Sin-disease is cunning, baffling, and powerful. And because of denial and delusion, one is oblivious to the fact that harmful attitudes and behaviors at once begin creeping back in to sabotage and destroy one's life and relationships. Suddenly, after a period of peace and serenity, I have found myself shouting at people I love or cutting them down with sarcasm, or lying to them, bewildered at the irrational turn the relationship is taking before my eyes.

When I don't get help and discuss my problems in a group I continue to blame what happens at such times on other people or circumstances. Alone, I will inevitably fall into fear of the future, self-pity, self-justification, self-righteousness, or a controlling self-will. That's why I must have other surrendering pilgrims I can call to share with when things get anxious and crazy in my mind.

The Disease Is Progressive

I am convinced that with the act of turning our lives over to God comes a greatly *increased* activity of our Sin. It's as if it were fighting for its life. And when the Disease is not confronted effectively, people seem invariably to get *more* selfish and self-centered as they get older.

Recently in a conference on small groups an older man challenged the idea that a Christian can't go it alone. He said, "You mean to tell me that God can't give a person all the growth he needs alone, I mean just between God and me?" I told him that I thought it was possible that God *could* do that, but that according to the Bible and the church's history, he has *chosen* to give us the church to grow in. Christ said he would be with us especially when two or three of us are gathered in his name (Matt. 18:20)

In any case, after twenty-nine years of periodically trying it on my own, I am convinced that it is impossible for *me* to go it alone if I want continuing sanity, change, growth, and discovery. And the delightful surprise is that now I look forward to attending the group meetings.

My Early Experience of Group Support

During the first four years after I made a commitment to God on the roadside in Texas I had no "Group" as such. I stayed alive spiritually by teaching a class of high school students at church. I decided to teach them the Bible. I had gone to seminary at one time and so had a pretty good background. I had been reading the Bible and devotional books and praying alone when I was asked to teach this class.

As I began to tell the Bible story to those young people, I also slipped in a little of what had happened to me. I told them about the changes I was experiencing each week because I was trying to commit my life to God. By having a place to report what was happening to me in my own spiritual journey (I wasn't telling anyone else), I began to have more faith and confidence and could feel a sense that I was being helped to grow—even though I would not have thought those young people would be able to give me much advice or "help."

But as they simply listened to what I said, asked about my life, and shared their questions and feelings, something very important was happening to *me*. I gained the courage to make some important changes in my behavior I'd never been able to make alone. When I was away from the class I found that the memory of their presence gave me courage. And sometimes the fact that I was going to be with them the next week kept me from giving up or chickening out and doing some of the unhealthy things I was trying to quit. For example, one Sunday I told them that God seemed to be telling me to take more time to listen to my family. The following week I was very busy when my wife asked me a question. I was just putting my coat on to dash out the front door to an appointment when I remembered what I had told the class. And I stopped and listened thoughtfully to what my wife was saying. I saw that in some way God was using what I had told those teenagers as a way to reach *me* with the message I'd shared with them.

Besides, when they shared out of their own experience I noticed that what they said about life was often very wise. For example, their comments concerning King David's struggles to be God's person and yet to get what he wanted that was not right revealed a real understanding of the issues of Sin and denial. Although those young people didn't know it, their listening and sharing helped keep the flame of faith alive in my own life and helped me to grow.

Later I met some adults who had made serious personal commitments to God and who could explain to me something of what had happened in my life when I'd begun trying to commit it to him. As I met with these people over coffee or sometimes in prayer groups at lunch or in the morning in business situations, I found that their struggles, their inability to "do it right," and the solutions they tried were a help to me when I failed. I didn't feel so discouraged when I realized that *everyone* who's trying to surrender his or her real life evidently has trouble living for God. Everyone has trouble keeping his or her selfishness and Sin-disease from blotting out any God-ward directions life might be taking.

The sharing of what was working for one of us was a great help to the rest. As I heard struggling new Christians report what was going on in their lives, I learned that everyone has to repent again and again. We all have to turn back to God in contrition, asking his forgiveness, surrendering in faith, and refocusing our lives on the day at hand. Luther called this sort of interchange "the mutual conversation of Christians" and maintained that God gave himself to us in (1) the Word, (2) the sacraments, and (3) the mutual conversation of Christians.

What would a small group look like that was structured for doing battle against the Disease?

21

Creating an Ongoing Recovery Group

I n the next two chapters I am going to describe
what goes on in a kind of group meeting that I
find necessary for my own survival and growth as I
continue to try to confront the Sin-disease and learn
how to live for God. I am not suggesting that other
kinds of Bible study and prayer groups are not valuable or that they should not continue. But I am convinced that if we are serious about confronting the
Disease in our lives and congregations we will have to
find and use *specific* ways to do that. If we stop with
mere verbal commitments and statements of intention, the Sin-disease will continue to eat us up.

The Ongoing Recovery Group

The "recovery" group is a meeting that helps us deal
primarily with the sins and character defects we can

see in our lives. For example, what do I do when I am afraid because of financial reversals and am tempted to forget about my commitment to God and go back to trying to solve my own problems? What do I do when I wake up feeling worthless or anxious and am tempted to act out immoral or selfish fantasies? What about when I feel angry at my wife or a close friend and alienate them and can't understand why they don't understand my point of view?

I was told that I could get real help for threatening life problems like these by getting into a group of surrendering people who were also trying to recover and learn to live for God.

Can Untrained People Give Really Valuable Help?

The question immediately came up in my mind (and often comes up when people are considering joining such a group): Can people with no theological or psychological training really help each other overcome serious character defects? For years I would have said no. But as I have participated in and watched groups operate over the years I have come to realize that a group of ordinary people trying to surrender their lives to God and discover their own denial and delusion with rigorous honesty can often give amazingly effective help with real-life difficulties.

Wisdom about living comes out of the hot caldron of pain. When a person has been in the thick of the soup with the Disease and has found a way to cope and live with a certain problem, that person's shared experience has three very important characteristics:

(1) It is authentic and concrete and can be identified with by another person in the midst of the same problem. (2) One can observe the solution and see how it's working in a real life. (3) *All* solutions and directions found are immediately assimilable without translation, because they are couched in the language of experience and behavior. Even the best theoretical advice has to be translated into action, and this is not an easy translation. (When I'm trying to translate a truth from a book or theory into *my* life and things don't work out, I'm never sure whether the theory failed or I "got it wrong.")

What is shared in a recovery group each week is often more wisdom about how to live than one could extract from much counseling or from reading an entire book.[1]

Not Looking for "Answers"

Two of my major character defects are self-righteousness and grandiosity. I hate to be "proved wrong" or told what to do in order to straighten out my life. When friends or family tried to tell me directly what I was doing wrong, I got angry and defensive, which just raised the walls of my denial. I couldn't hear what they were telling me. So when I finally got the courage to bring up a problem in a group, I wasn't really asking for an "answer" to my problems. I didn't want someone else to tell me what I "should" do. I had hidden my sins and feelings in the first place because I hadn't been able to change them. I felt shame about my self-centeredness and failure to "do it right" and to be "perfect" or "sinless." Even as a surrendering person I still sometimes feel judged and hopeless when the Disease has me. And I am angered and afraid when someone tries to "straighten me out" in a group by *telling* me how I *should* have behaved. I do that sort of judgmental "helping" enough to myself.

What I wanted was to know how other people handled the same problems in their *own* lives—leaving me free to "try on" their solutions to see if they fit my circumstances. So I was greatly relieved to discover that this is how good recovery groups operate. People don't "give advice." They share their experience, strength, and hope as they deal with their specific failures, problems, and successes and the strong feelings they experience. When someone shares with stark honesty the ways they have tried to cope with the same problems that I'm facing in my life, a light comes on in the room for me. An aura of serenity seeps into the group as they share the pain and the helpful and strengthening experiences along with the problems. Some of the rest of us can identify and sometimes see the same difficulties that have been hidden from our own view. Often at the moment of "seeing" we can discover practical ways we might cope with the same issue.

For example, today (the day I am writing this) I realized in a recovery group that the reason I get angry at people close to me when they don't understand what I am saying to them is that when I was a small boy my mother (now dead) used to question what I was saying by interrupting me with the comment, "I don't understand what you're saying." (What she really meant was, "You are not saying it *right*. And if you think *that* [the opinion I had just expressed] I can't accept you.") Today I remembered those scenes as a little boy and how I quickly altered what I'd said to get her approval. But I remembered feeling anger and fear at being manipulated and threatened with rejection—even though I didn't understand how it was happening at the time.

As an adult I still get "irrationally" angry when someone in my family does not understand what I am saying—because I feel as though I am about to be manipulated again. But in fifty-nine years I never saw the reason for my anger until someone else in a recovery group told of frustration in trying to communicate with a parent.

I was overjoyed to realize that this recurring irrational anger did not mean I was crazy. It had a starting place in real pain in my childhood. I saw that the people around me are not "purposely" misunderstanding me. Also I now know that my Sin sometimes skews my personal communications.

Regardless of other people's intentions, I now believe I can begin to change my behavior with God's help. I see that I don't have to allow people to manipulate me—so I don't have to get angry even when I think they might try to. When I foul up I know I can make amends with integrity to the people close to me about my anger attacks because I am not doomed to repeat the process forever.

Since different people have certain problems at different stages in their recovery from the Disease, almost everyone can be both helper and helped. I noticed a relaxed serenity and a lot of wisdom in the members of these groups who had been around awhile.

However, in meetings where people tried to give advice and "fix up" those who expressed problems and failures, the ones who had risked sharing real issues were driven away. In those nonvulnerable, advice-giving groups there was very little peace, joy, or wisdom; the Disease and its insidious denied character defects seemed to be virtually untouched.

Rigorous Honesty or Spiritual Death—the Long-Range Choice

I am convinced that the fear of facing real feelings is almost universal. All my life my own fear of facing anger, fear, guilt, loneliness, hurt, and other feelings accompanying failure and Sin had made the kind of spiritual growth that leads to authentic character change impossible for me. I had a real fear of having people know my faults. I'd spent a lot of years trying to "do it right." My wife seemed to see that I wasn't all that perfect, but in my delusion I thought that she saw more faults than were there for some reason. And in groups—although I didn't know about denial then—I had a lot of fear that "they" might find something about me *I* couldn't stand to see, or have them see.

I now know that unless I can let other people *see* my failures and my feelings about them, my brothers and sisters in recovery have no way to love me and help me through those failures.

Personal Growth Problems Not Solved with Quick Answers

If someone immediately quotes a Scripture or gives advice to every difficulty or feeling expressed (instead of identifying with the problem and sharing from his or her own life), the person presenting the issue will be quickly trained (without anything having been said about it out loud) that one "*cannot* be a first-class person in this group" if one continues to have problems, failures, and "inappropriate feelings."

The biblical truth, however, is that people who try to surrender their lives to God will continue to have failures and problems as long as they are alive and growing! (See again Paul's description of the continuing Christian struggle with "hidden reality" in Rom. 7:7–25 quoted in part in chapter 8. He follows that description with an urging to let God fill us with his spirit. And I have sensed God's spirit as people abandon themselves to him and get real.)

New growth brings to awareness new difficulties as well as new joys. As the walls of unreality crack open, problems never faced before come seeping (or leaping) into consciousness and must be dealt with. My experience indicates that groups that cannot handle sins and authentic feelings of anger, fear, and pain will simply fade and die spiritually. A spirit of boredom will set in, or at least a lack of enthusiasm, and the Disease will remain in control.

The Bible and the church's history indicate that we *must* learn to be rigorously honest with God, each other, and ourselves or we will stagnate spiritually.

Jesus implied, perhaps with no little sarcasm, that even God cannot heal us unless we know we need a physician (see Matt. 9:12 and 13).

Membership

The membership of the group we are about to look at is open and ongoing. It is flexible as to size. The members may range from three or four to twenty or even more. Since each person will usually be reporting on how he or she faces *one* particular issue each week, the group can be much larger than the usual small group and everyone who wants to can still participate. The requirements for membership in a recovery group are the same as the first steps in the surrendering process: an awareness that we are powerless to change by ourselves, a belief that God can restore us to sanity, and a desire to turn our will and our whole lives over to God.

What I have always tried to do when I call people together for a new group is to tell them that this is an experiment and will perhaps be different for some of them. I tell them that *I* really need a place to come to talk for one hour a week about the specific details of how to live for God. Not only do I need a place to talk about my failures and my joys, but I need to learn how to deal with the character defect problems, the resentments, fears, and angers that continually block me in my attempts to love God and the people around me—including me. I tell them that I am going to set out some ground rules that have been helpful to peo-

ple in the past as they have tried to create conditions
for living as God's people.

Ground Rule Conditions

1. The first condition is confidentiality. *What is said
in this meeting stays here!* If trust is going to develop,
the things shared by group members *must* be kept
confidential. The most effective groups require membership confidentiality—so that people don't divulge
who attends meetings.

2. The second condition is that people who want
to enter the experiment of this group must have decided that they are powerless to fix their lives up alone
and want to consider letting God help them to wholeness and sanity. The initial group should be made up
of people who have already decided to try to give their
lives to God. Later, new people can be brought in who
have suspected their powerlessness and are willing to
consider that God may be the answer to their condition.
They may not be able to make any promises about
"being good" or changing their habits; in fact, no one
can guarantee to keep such promises. (The Bible is
clear that we're not to swear that we will do anything,
because by ourselves we can't change a hair of our
heads (Matt. 5:36).)

That is part of our awareness of being powerless.
But the intention must be for all of the members of
the group to be committed to giving God back the
central position in their lives and to accepting him as
the primary meaning and power for living. In the

group we intend to find out who we were made to be each day and what character defects are keeping us from being those people. We want to finish dealing with our past, and to discover what we can do in order to participate in his will in the world in the present day.

We are not promising to "do it right." We are merely committing ourselves to pray and to try to be willing to make the character changes necessary to live with God as the center of our existence. We will keep trying to remember that we are aiming at progress as a way of life, not an unrealistic perfection.

The leadership for each meeting can be passed from member to member after the group is well established. But to lead, a person should have been solidly in a program of recovery for at least three months (although this may be impossible in a beginning group).

Content: Specific Problems and Positive Discoveries

The content of the group is the *specific* problems of living and feelings about them. As participants we are to share our experiences, strengths, and hope with each other regarding these problems.

To begin each session the leader may want to lead the group in a short prayer like the following by Reinhold Niebuhr:

"Lord, grant me the serenity to accept the things I cannot change, the courage to change the things I can, and the wisdom to know the difference."

Following the prayer the leader asks if there are any new people. If there are he or she welcomes them and asks them to give their first names, telling them that this is a group for people who have recognized their inordinate self-centeredness and are trying to surrender their whole lives to God.

Then the leader might ask someone to read the ground rules (given earlier in this chapter).

After that reading the leader asks if anyone has a specific problem to discuss and get help with. (If there are new people in the meeting the leader should consider strongly having the subject be, How did you become aware that you were powerless and decide to turn to God? Each old member can respond and perhaps help everyone deal with powerlessness again.) If, after a period of silence, no one responds with a suggestion for a topic, the leader tells his or her name and suggests a problem. (It often helps if the leader waits in silence thirty seconds or more before suggesting a problem topic, since it may take people awhile to have the courage to state a problem.)

If no one states an issue, the leader should. For instance, the leader for the meeting (let's say his name is Jack) might bring up one of the beginning steps toward recovery mentioned earlier (e.g., recognition of powerlessness, realization that God can bring us back to sanity, committing our lives and wills to God, or prayer, worship, confession, or Bible reading). Jack can then talk about the trouble he had doing it and/ or mention something that helped when he was trying to surrender or make room in his life for doing whatever he's chosen to talk about. Or Jack can bring up any other problem he is facing that is getting in the way of his recovery from the Disease.

He could say, for example, "My name is Jack Smith. Tonight I'd like to talk about 'anxiety.' What do you do when you are anxious?"

And then Jack can begin by describing his own experience with anxiety and what he does when the problem strikes. Jack tells specifically what he experiences when anxiety hits him—the fear ("the tightness in my chest" or the "nauseated feeling in my stomach"), the desire to run away or to get angry with people close to him, perhaps the desire to eat or drink or work so he can "forget" his anxiety and not have to face the painful feelings it brings. Then he tells the group exactly what he *does* to deal with the anxiety (such as admit his powerlessness and resurrender his life to God, call a group member, call his minister, read a certain book or Scripture passage, etc.).

It may be that Jack has a very positive "solution" that often works for him. Or it may be that he has the problem a lot and hasn't found much to do but come to meetings, pray, and wait it out. It is not necessary to have a "positive solution" to be helpful. As a matter of fact I am sometimes strengthened most when someone has the same problem I'm facing and is stuck in it but still taking the necessary steps to get help. Above all, the group should *not* try to "fix Jack up" and tell him what he should do. The *stating* of a problem has real healing value and relieves much stress.

But when the leader has stated and described a problem he can call on some of the old-timers who've been trying to do God's will the longest to tell their experiences in dealing with anxiety and what they do when it hits. Then Jack can continue to call on people, or ask if anyone else would like to talk about anxiety. Or he can nod to the person to his left and go around the room letting the people who haven't spoken share their experiences with anxiety and how they cope with it as they try to live committed to God. If new members can just state their first names and/or perhaps say they have the problem but don't know much to do about it, they will be helped. This is one of the wonders of this sort of interaction.

Every person states his or her first name before sharing. The stating of names is important in that it helps new people get acquainted faster, and it identifies the person speaking with the problem so everyone knows that there are no "perfect" people present. After giving his or her name, the group member goes on to tell how he or she faces the problem stated in his or her own life.

Some groups use an adapted form of the Twelve Steps of Alcoholics Anonymous as a part of their recovery (see the Appendix for a list adapted for fighting the Sin-disease). When this is the case, someone working on a particular step may share how that helped with the problem being discussed.

If someone comes up with a solution that seems *in*effective to someone else, the second person does *not* "set the first one straight." *No one* knows what another may need to hold him-or herself together for the time being. As each person shares what works for him or her, the ones having "ineffective" solutions may begin to see the picture and change on their own, whereas if they are "straightened out" by a strong person, the whole group may quit sharing. The purpose of this group is not giving advice or getting other people to change. It is for *us* to change *ourselves*. We are to listen, take what is helpful to us and leave the rest without comment or argument and have effective strategies for coping with them is a very positive experience for persons struggling with similar life problems.

Since the primary characteristic of Sin is denial, a group member may not see that he or she has the problem that is being discussed. Yet it may be apparent to others in the group that the problem is a major issue in that person's life. But unless the one in denial *asks* for feedback it is often better not to confront the Disease at that level in this sort of group. There are other kinds of groups in which this sort of feedback is an integral part, but their description is beyond the scope of this book.

A few minutes before the set closing time for the group the leader can ask if anyone has anything to say before the meeting is over. This can be very beneficial to someone who has come with a bottled-up problem but couldn't get it said during the meeting, or someone who has had an important insight that he or she feels a strong need to share. The group may want to close the meeting by holding hands and praying the Lord's Prayer together.

These meetings (which often last one hour) can help a great deal in the spiritual recovery and growth processes. Many people will see denied behaviors and character defects as others share their problems and experiences. But the Disease will not give up easily, and there are some common problems that may come up and sabotage the group's life.*

*For information about starting a group based on these principles, write Sinners Anonymous Service Center, P.O. Box 26001, Austin, TX 78755–0001

22

Problems in Groups

It has been important for me to discover the great resistance many people, especially religious people, have to seeing that denial even exists for them. My own stubborn defensiveness helped me to realize the tremendous strength of this resistance. It is not easy for me to admit that I am truly self-centered and that I continue to engage in anxious and harmful behavior that only God can deal with successfully. If we are not fully aware of the strength and tenacity of this resistance to seeing the effects of Sin in our lives, we will be continually surprised when fellow group members keep trying in various ways to move the group away from confronting the Sin-disease. As a matter of fact, group members who are threatened (consciously or unconsciously) will often keep complaining about "all this negativism" or ask, "Why aren't we studying the Bible?" until they either break up the group or get the content into the safer waters of some sort of cognitive study or nonvulnerable "prayer group" format. Both of those are necessary and helpful for spiritual growth, but not in recovery groups. Yet unfortunately this resistance and the deterioration of the group that follows if it is not handled well is the story of most of the groups I have been in, at least before I learned what I have just written here.

It is important to realize that resistance is sometimes a *necessary* and *healthy* thing and should be respected. Some people are far too fragile for some of the sharing and encounters we are discussing here; they do not yet have enough ego strength to deal with such dynamics. So it is good to respect resistance whenever it arises and give people a chance to leave the group without embarrassment (or criticism from the other members). From the beginning it is good to point out that "this group is not for everyone and some may choose to leave—and that's OK." (There is another kind of resistance that is a part of rebellion dynamics, but this sort of group is not the place to deal with the kind of intervention that may require. If a kind and direct approach setting out the ground rules for this kind of group doesn't work, the only recourse may be to suggest to the person rebelling that this is obviously not the right group for him or her.)

Trouble in a Group

Trouble in a group can come at any point. I think that one who is starting a new group should realize that Sin is working constantly to destroy the group through *any* member's diseased behaviors—including his or her own. Sometimes the one who started the group may have become arrogant and not want to pass the leadership around or may have begun dealing with problems in such a way that the other members of the group are bored or feel that the group has quit being honest or sensitive. He or she may have a know-it-all attitude and be giving advice instead of sharing.

It is very difficult to maintain an atmosphere of intimacy and to continue to be particular and specific about the difficulties, joys, hopeful experiences, and honest feelings involved in living and trying to recover. So it is good if the group members can face these problems openly. But most people simply will not risk that sort of confrontation at first.

Sometimes after weeks of real sharing and growth something happens and the group just seems to "seal over" and quit being intimate. The talk is impersonal, with little or no expression of the *feelings* of the members. The group's conversation may drift to the price of silver on the market or some aspect of current national politics. (That's why it's valuable to read the group's purposes at each meeting.) But when this shutting down of the expressing of feelings happens and the leader does not have the courage and the insight to face the problem with the group, it is often just as well if the group is allowed to dissolve. The hope is that the members will need the group enough to fight for it, and when they do, they will bring up the unreality and stop it by starting to be real again themselves.

Dealing with a Blocked Group

Here is one way to deal with a blocked group. It is sometimes helpful if the leader or another member can say, "I sense that we are not being personal. As a matter of fact, I am not being personal and honest myself. I fear that the group is losing its power to help me, and I really don't know what to do about it. I wonder if any of you have similar feelings about what has happened to us?" Then let the other people around the room talk. Sometimes a group can be reborn again and again through that experience as the members confess their fears, frustrations, and feelings of resentment and closedness. Such "group consciousness" sessions can be helpful in solving any problems that surface. The wisdom of the group is often very effective and inhibits any one member from trying to impose his or her will on the entire group.

Sometimes confronting the leader or another member with the fact that he or she is giving advice and not sharing can help that person immensely. This too is done best by members expressing their own feelings instead of engaging in an attack on the ability or character of the leader. We are all in the same half-healed state. In recovery groups we are all *always* only wounded healers.

One of the reasons for having ground rules for a group is to help when trouble starts. But the best approach—whatever the problem—is to stay with your own feelings and not to point judgmental fingers. It is much more effective to say, "When you said (or did) that I felt fear and anger," than to say, "You're being judgmental, and I resent the hell out of your trying to push us around!" Honesty concerning the group members' feelings about what is happening will often get through best. Remember constantly that we are *all* only in the process of recovering from Sin and are vulnerable to jumping back into our old self-centered and controlling behavior.

Shutting Down a Group

Groups will last different lengths of time. My own experience has been that some people get in a group for a while and then either sense they need to go to another place or get discouraged and decide to quit. At one time Andrea and I were in a group of people who met together for a couple of years. Finally one morning we were sitting in our home alone, and no one showed up. When that happened two weeks in a row, we realized that the group was over.

There is a tendency to feel rejected when that happens, but I have realized that groups are often just for a period of time in which people become conscious of their need to come together and grow. Sometimes they continue for years, but other times the felt needs of different group members change, and they quit. Sometimes people feel threatened when they get close to seeing their Sin or denial or by the changes they sense God is calling them to make in their lives—especially relative to their compulsive or addictive behaviors—and they move away from the group.

When some of these things happen to a number of

people, I now feel free to let the group end and move on. I think that sometimes people are reluctant to *ever* close down any kind of group that has been officially started, for fear people may think the group is failing or rejecting them. But groups are not ends in themselves. A group is just a means and a place for people to meet and grow—to live out, to enflesh, the biblical good news that dealt a fatal blow to Sin and death. When the situation changes and people no longer feel a need for the group, often the best thing to do is let it die. That way something else can be born in its place that will meet people where they are. Because of my own need for a group, I have had to keep finding one (or starting a new one) wherever I've been.

I suspect that there will always be problems in groups, but until God shows me a better way to recover, I'll probably keep being a part of them.

V

Moving Beyond
Ourselves

23

Telling Other People About the Hope of Recovery

Sharing the news that there is hope for recovery from the fear, guilt, shame, and compulsive behavior caused by Sin is not as simple as it sounds.

Since the Disease's primary weapons are denial and delusion, people "out there" in the grips of Sin do not know that they need to be in recovery. They don't realize the extent to which they're being controlled by the Disease. For example, a woman may be a vicious gossip, a constant manipulator and controller of her family, friends, and any organization of which she is a part. People begin drifting away from her, and she finally comes to the point where she is no longer invited to parties or to be a part of any organization. No one calls her. Her grown children never write and seldom come home, and her husband is always "working," or at least gone from home when he can manage it. Yet it still has not occurred to her that she has or is a problem. In her Sin-blindness she only believes she is surrounded by selfish, insensitive people.

In the case of a person whose Disease is manifested by addiction to a chemical, it is often true that even losing family and job and being in jail on a second drunk-driving charge—all because of drinking—will not cause that person to realize and admit that he or she has a problem with alcohol. Everyone else can see it plainly.

To such people, sharing the fact that "help is available" isn't often effective or even welcome. That is, it isn't welcome *until* a person reaches a place at which the problems caused by the Disease can't be solved by his or her best thinking and most strenuous efforts. As I suggested earlier, most people never make serious changes in their lives until the alternative is to lose something they feel they cannot do without (family, job, reputation, freedom, sanity, peace of mind).

What Kind of Communication Unlocks the Gate in the Wall of Denial?

Anyone who has dealt with the carnage of the Disease knows that a frontal attack on denial only thickens the walls.

There are many different ways to communicate hope to people whose Sin is making their lives miserable, but there seems to be one primary approach that oils the hinges and helps suffering people to "open the gate" and walk out from behind their walls of repression.

This most practical kind of communication comes from recovering sinners sharing their experience, strength, and hope with those not yet in recovery. Someone who has seen his or her own denied self-centeredness and crippling behaviors knows a secret that the person not in recovery doesn't know. The secret is what it feels like to be on *both* sides of the walls of denial and delusion. For example, John, a recovering man, might go to another man who is near the end of his rope. John can tell the sufferer about how he, John, struggled and failed to be able to make things right in his own life. John can describe the growing fear, the acid stomach, the shame about not being able to stop his self-defeating behavior and straighten things out in his life, the aching loneliness, the anger and frustration in the long nights, and the sense of isolation and worthlessness. John can tell about how someone helped him see that he was powerless over the Disease or he would have been able to fix things in his life before. John can tell how he resisted seeing his own selfishness and blamed everything on other people but then came to realize that he really did have a problem and that *he* and *his selfishness* were indeed the cause of his misery.

If the person doesn't ask "What happened?" at this point and changes the subject, then John lets it go. John is not there to manipulate or "sell." But if the man he's speaking to does say, "What did you do then?" John can share how he was told that if he would turn his will and his life over to God, God would give him the power to overcome his selfishness and his compulsive behavior and live a new life—one day at a time. He didn't have to understand much about God, but began by making the decision on the basis of what he could understand. And John can tell about the sense of hope and serenity he has found as he has come together with other surrendering people and tried to take the steps necessary to recover from the Sin-disease.

John is in no way judging the other person or taking his inventory. John is just talking about his *own* Sin and the hope he is finding in recovery. It may be that the other man is not ready to admit that he has a problem he can't handle. And that should present no difficulty for John, since he's not trying to "get results." In fact, John is telling the other person for John's own sake, because he knows that only by sharing the good news of recovery can one keep it over the long haul. So there's no pressure to succeed or convince people that they need God. The *act* of sharing one's experience, strength, and hope is enough. The rest is up to God and the other person.

But even if some people who are in obvious trouble don't receive what John has to say at the time and keep careening down the hallways of their lives bouncing off the walls, some day when they hit the end and collapse in a heap of despair they may remember what John said. And because John shared and didn't preach at them they may come back to him for guidance.

But if the man in the example does respond to John and says, "Yeah, that's what's happening to me," John can take him to a recovery meeting and introduce him to other people who are trying to release the unhealthy control of their lives to God. John can tell him how he can make a decision to turn his own will and life over to God to get the power to overcome the deadly self-lock of Sin. John can share with him this book, or if he has a specific addiction or compulsion, John can get him a book on overeating, alcohol addiction, or whatever the compulsion is. And in these ways John can help the suffering person into recovery and a new life among God's people.

Intervention

I will mention one other kind of intentional communication that can be very effective in helping people get through denial: intervention. It is often a powerful tool in helping people get through especially stubborn resistance to seeing the reality of their lives—people who are wrecking their own and other people's lives by their compulsive, diseased behavior. Intervention sometimes crashes through entrenched defenses with "tough love," so that the one being helped can see the serious consequences of the Disease's operation in his or her own life and relationships.

The idea of intervention (several people going to someone who has sinned against somebody else but who can't see it or won't admit it) is a biblical principle described briefly in Matthew 18:15–16. Interventions are now used almost exclusively in the chemical dependency field to confront people who are in denial about their addiction to alcohol or drugs. For a description of that sort of intervention, see the book *I'll Quit Tomorrow.*[1] *Warning: Do not do an intervention without prior training and an experienced person to conduct it!* This is a powerful tool but dangerous to relationships. *Prior* to the intervention there should be a definite plan for recovery recommended by a professional counselor.

Some "Rules of Thumb" Concerning Sharing the News of Hope

I'm convinced that in every case it is *God* who finally gets through people's defensive walls so they can see that they really aren't the self-contained and all-powerful person (able to handle all their own problems) that the Disease tells them they are. But when a person has turned life over to God and sees his or her own delusion, then sooner or later it is almost as if God furnishes that person a new set of eyes to see his or her behavior as it really is. The surrendered also can see other people hiding from the same kinds of pain, lostness, and searching they have experienced. It may be that such people can go and stand with others in their pain. It may be that they can ask the hurting ones if they would like a way out of their pain and confusion. Each person can find an appropriate way to ask this question and then to tell the story of the mess, confusion, and pain that led to considering "giving up" to God. But initially I believe it is best to go with an old-timer to see how to approach people without scaring them away.

At first there is a real danger of the newly recovering person coming on as an arrogant know-it-all. I hate it when someone has just gone to a conference or read a book (which I haven't read) and tells me how "wonderful" it is in a way that makes me feel "out of it," as if the present hope I am clinging to is inadequate. People like that seem to be implying that if I only knew what they now know, I would be a first-class person. But as it is—well, they're just sorry I couldn't make it to the conference, or read the book. That kind of insensitive enthusiasm often makes other people withdraw and feel hurt and rejected—and *angry*—since it feels like judgment.

Keeping One's Mouth Shut for God's Sake

The only way I know to avoid this is for the new person in recovery to keep his or her mouth shut about the "crucial nature of the new surrender." (See Jesus' advice to the man who had been healed to "tell no one," Mark 7:36.) For a while I believe it's enough to talk only to other people who are on the adventure and in recovery groups about the "life-changing insights" that have been coming. For one thing, many people who begin to live their lives for God in the way I am describing drop away after an encounter or two with the Disease. Before you start sharing the life of recovery, it's a good idea to make sure you want to stay in it.

With Family and Friends

In relationships with family and friends I'm finding that for me it's often better to listen and love these people on their own terms. This means being interested in *them* instead of oneself and one's own spiritual pilgrimage when talking to them. This may sound contradictory to the usual injunction to "spread the word." (If you want to try what I'm suggesting, go from your reading of this book and ask members of your family how they've been—and then listen to what they tell you. Then they'll know you've changed.)

Before spreading the word to anyone, I've found it's helpful to listen, and to watch and learn from old-timers. Yet even knowing this, it is still hard for me to keep from "preaching it."

At first I felt I could shortcut this listening-learning-seasoning process, and I've offended some fine people in my overeagerness to help them. For instance, when I found out about my own hiding of awareness, other members of my family did not take kindly to my "tentative and subtle" suggestions that they too might not be facing some of the denied issues in *their* lives. Before talking to anyone I needed to learn how to love and respect God and other people as they were, as I soaked in the new life of recovery. And that takes some time.

For me this approach is not just a matter of intellectual understanding. As a matter of fact, an academic education is often a hindrance to recovery. My own training in theology and psychology make it very difficult for me to truly surrender and trust in the areas of my greatest fears and insecurities. I have a huge need to "control by understanding"—which doesn't work with the Disease. The only doorways I've seen through the walls of my denial and delusion are admission of powerlessness, turning my life over to God every day, guts, rigorous honesty, feedback, self-examination, confession, and making amends. This way of change is more of a "learning by osmosis," a process of going to meetings and doing the things I've suggested, day after day. I've come to believe that recovery is a lot more like making pickles then learning sums. You can't make a pickle by painting a cucumber with salt water. You've got to soak 'em in it.

Not a "Quick Fix" Cure

In this book I'm not talking about a new small group program rewarmed from the sixties. The way of recovery is an ongoing life-and-death struggle—in which we keep reenacting and claiming God's "win" over Sin each time we abandon ourselves anew and each time we participate in the communion. As we get in touch with our feelings, it is often fear we feel, so the way of recovery necessarily includes a lot of fearful feelings.

Every day Sin is nudging people toward divorce, child and spouse abuse, angry separations between parents and grown children, sex crimes, and addictions to alcohol, drugs (including tranquilizers and sleeping pills), sex, and food—not to mention neurotic addictions to work, money, people-pleasing, "people-fixing," and religion. As I mentioned earlier, any of these spiritual-behavior symptoms can cause a person serious physical symptoms, even death.

If You're in a Church

I found it helpful to go to my minister and simply tell him that I was trying to make a serious surrender of my life to God and that I wanted to recover from the compulsive and diseased behaviors that had caused me so much trouble in my relationships with God and people. I told him that although things might have appeared to be going well in my life, I had discovered that I was powerless to change certain harmful behaviors and specific emotional and spiritual habits. I told him that the results of these behaviors were tearing me up inside; I had seen that I could not "think" my way out of these problems and was committing all of my future I could to God. This had given me a whole new set of issues in my life to work on. I asked the minister for his prayers, guidance about books and groups that might be helpful, and other kinds of support. And I've felt a lot closer to him since I did this.

If your minister is critical or derisive, that's another matter. You may have to forgo talking about your new life with such a person. You may have to simply go on with your group and learn all you can about how to be God's person in your situation. But I would suspect most ministers will respond positively and gratefully to the news that people in the flock are making a serious attempt to commit their whole lives to God and face their Sin. Such ministers can give one a lot of support and love.

Not a Popular Way

The kind of surrender and continual confrontation of the Disease that we are discussing are not emphasized in all churches. People who espouse this attempt at rigorously honest living appear to many to be pushing another of the fads that sweep through history periodically, leaving division and spiritual bruises everywhere in their wake.

So if you try this way of recovery from Sin, I strongly advise you to live it quietly awhile before trying to spread it at all. I've found that if my life changes, people will wonder why. If it doesn't, why should they care what I've discovered? In any case, my job is only to face and deal with my *own* Sin, not theirs.

But to complete the cure I must learn to do more than talk about it.

24

"Completing" the Cure: Giving It Away

The Bible says, "Faith by itself, if it has no works, is dead" (James 2:17). And my experience has been confirmed by what someone told me recently, "Willingness without action is fantasy."

The most vulnerable point I've found in the armor of my Sin is that it cannot seem to control me when I'm focused on helping someone else without expecting a payoff. So for me, giving away the personal touch and the message of God's care, forgiveness, and power to help us is a necessity if I plan to recover and stay alive spiritually.

I know now that I am not "cured" from Sin, even though I am consciously trying to surrender my life to God every day. So "completing the cure" is not a totally accurate way of speaking. What I have is a daily reprieve from powerlessness, a reprieve that is contingent on my giving today to God *and* trying to take the vision of his will and his love into every activity, every relationship in my life. When I try to do this, however hesitantly or inadequately, things are better for me and, I suspect, for those around me.

But I am so self-centered that this focusing on God, and especially other people, has been almost impossible for me. I *forget* about helping other people and put off making calls or seeking out those who are sick or in trouble and going to see them. When I first began—and sometimes still—I would decide to call on someone in the morning and forget all about it until the next morning . . . or the next week.

Several times I almost gave up and said to God, "Well, Lord, I'm just not the helping type. Maybe I could increase my giving to charity?" But as I watched people who appeared to be really recovering from the Disease and growing into authentic men and women, I noticed that all of them were personally involved in helping people *face to face* (not just putting a check in the mail). And they told me, "It's OK to give money and to serve on boards, but to stay in recovery and to grow in serenity, we've found that we've got to help other people personally who are in the grips of the Disease. We've got to let them know that when they become powerless and alone, God is waiting to give them his power and love to help them get well." And to do that we have to be with them somehow.

Back to Life-Sized Living

Years ago I had started out that way when I made my first serious and specific commitment to God as an adult. I spent hours listening to people and telling them about the hope I was finding in God. But the years went by, and I began to travel and speak and write books. I figured that since I was speaking to a lot of people at seminars, I had to get some rest from people when I got home. So I made myself less and less available to people I didn't know in the town where I lived.

It was *true* that I couldn't do all the traveling I was doing, have a family life, *and* spend much time helping people personally in our town. But I was so grandiose that it didn't occur to me to *cut out* some of the speaking and do the personal contacting I now know I needed for my own spiritual health.

So when I finally saw my powerlessness and got a glimpse of my delusion, I realized that my life had to change a lot if I were going to stay alive spiritually in recovery. As I abandoned my future to God and began taking an inventory of my life, I saw that *for me* the constant traveling and speaking had been a way to avoid facing the everyday feelings and character defects that made my life unmanageable. I decided to cancel my speaking commitments and not take on new ones for a while. (I actually stopped altogether for almost two years after I had recovered from the heart symptoms.)

I felt some fear and some withdrawal pains about not speaking. "What if people forgot about me?" "What if I wanted to speak later and no one would invite me?" The Disease seemed to light up all my insecurities, my fear of failure and other character defects, and to frighten me with them.

But now I had a program to work at and some friends to tell me that the Disease always attacks like that when people get serious about changing their lives.

A Halting First Step

At first I couldn't make myself reach out to people in our town. I realized that I was burned out on "talking about God." But my friends responded, "Who said anything about 'talking' God? We said, 'visiting the stranger' and 'helping people who are sick and in trouble.'"

I went to our minister and to a friend in the chemical dependency field and said I'd be glad to take people in trouble to the hospital if they needed someone to do that. (The hospital was forty miles from the town we lived in.) And they both took me up on my offer on several occasions.

Several months after my turning to God at dawn, I called on a couple of people who had signed the visitors' book at our church. I was quite resistant to doing this. I'm very shy inside and was afraid they would reject me. I just told them we were glad they had come to our church and hoped they'd come back. And I listened and found out a little about them. Before I left I gave them a church newsletter. Now, after many more months, I get the names of the visitors after church and try to visit them. (We belonged to a tiny mission when I began writing this book, and the numbers were not great.)

I usually felt so much better after those first visits that each morning I began to decide on *one* person I would try to contact that day (each day). I was not going to "talk theology," and the person might be a friend, family member, or stranger. I was just going to find out how they were—just contact them because God has done so much for *me*. Sometimes I make a phone call to a relative or friend, or I write a letter. Other days it's someone who is sick or grieving or who is trapped by an addiction or is afraid because of some crisis.

The discouraging thing to me has been that some weeks I might skip five days or even six. But the one or two contacts I did make represented a real change. I realized again that I am into progress and not the sick perfectionism of my past. Some days I have called on several people. Gradually I've seen that I'm changing the patterns of a lifetime.

And the surprising thing is that many of the people I contact start talking to me about their questions concerning God and problems family members are having. I also find that after many months of meeting with people in recovery groups that I am beginning to get involved with a few group members regarding problems they (and I) are facing. But I am setting up boundaries to keep from falling into my compulsive work addiction again. I have asked friends to tell me if they see me getting into my old habits. And as I have been trying to change my life to include people who are outside my usual self-centered world, I am feeling stronger in my *own* battle with the Disease.

Healthy Groups Nudge People Toward Loving Others

In recovery and growth groups in which people are really demonstrating recovery, sooner or later some of the members will sense a need to share the gifts they are receiving from God. They will want to get involved with helping people who are in trouble, with being peacemakers, with comforting the grieving, visiting the sick, helping with projects to feed the hungry, or to share God's love and message in various other ways in the world.

I think this is a sure sign that the group members are becoming healthy and are traveling with God. Ultimately I am convinced that the recovering person will reveal his or her faith through behavior more than words.

Moving Beyond the Group: Unselfishness Is Not an Option, But Neither Is Continuing Recovery

My advice would be to start *other* groups for the purpose of reaching out and keep one group where the primary purpose is staying well in the life of recovery.

This means that a group project to help people with their material needs or to contact them regarding their participation in the church or other religious institution will take an additional commitment, perhaps another meeting each week.

In one group I was in someone had an idea about turning part of the church into a free medical clinic during the week for people who could not afford medical services (yet had too much money to get free services from the government). Those who were interested were so excited and eager to do this project that talk about the new venture could have taken over and swamped our recovery group. A different group was formed, made up of people whose main focus and interest was the medical clinic. But those from our group didn't quit our meeting. They committed to additional meetings each week to carry out the new project.

There are all kinds of different ways men and women surrendering to God will feel touched to help others. My experience would indicate that it will be hard for some people to get out of old selfish habits to give time for the ordinary, nondramatic helping of other people. I'm afraid I wouldn't do it myself if my own spiritual recovery didn't depend on it.

The Fear of Writing This

I have fears about writing what you've just read. I am afraid it may be more of my exhibitionism—and that the Disease will try to convince me that having written about these things I don't have to *do* them any more. If I leave this material in the book it will be because I want very much to tell people that, for me, beginning to reach out to others to give away what one is finding doesn't mean mounting a full-fledged "evangelistic campaign" of some sort or starting a housing project for the poor or a treatment center. Although I don't rule out the possibility that God may eventually lead me to do something like that, I know that unless I keep contacting people face to face one day at a time, my Sin will win the battle for my life. For me, the beginning of recovery has meant quietly going and being present to people to whom God leads me— however he does it.

I'm also afraid to write these things because I don't know how long I will keep doing them. But all I am learning tells me that I am only responsible for living *this one day* for God. He will guide me and give me the strength to live for him tomorrow as I give *that* day to him and ask, "How can I serve you?" and tell him, "Thy will (not mine) be done."

As more time passed I joined a civic club for the first time in my life and I also became a member of a diocesan committee on evangelism in our church. These are not big things, but they represent great changes of focus in my life. Some people may find out they need to *give up* these sorts of activities and spend more time doing things at home or working at their vocation—as I may later.

With regard to my vocation, I am writing this book one day at a time. I'm not sure where God is going to lead me vocationally, but that doesn't seem so important today. I've spent a lot of my life in oversized dreams about the future, and with my "eyes on the horizon" have blindly trampled over the bodies of those around me who may have been crying out for attention and love. I don't want to live that way anymore.

When I began this book I talked about the anxieties and fears of trying to cope with problems and people who seemed intractable. I talked about powerlessness and unmanageability and Sin-filled behaviors. I still do not understand all the reasons my life gets snarled up in these things. But I do know that for me the doorway to recovery from Sin and a new experience of life came through trying to give the whole future to God and to live for him one day at a time.

On this side of that surrender—along with the very real pain of deaths and new births—are increasing periods of a kind of inner peace that echoes with joy and gladness.

Epilogue:
To the Reader

What I have been describing in this book is not a new thing: it came from the Bible originally. But the Sin-disease has been so powerful and effective that some of us religious folk have rejected the powerful tools that God originally gave us to combat the deceitful and denied Sin in our lives and institutions.

Again and again throughout history groups of men and women have been confronted and convicted of their Sin by God's Holy Spirit. And they have cried out to the rest of us that there is no hope of the peace and joy and power of God without surrender to him and rigorous honesty of life.

In our time the Twelve-Step programs have sprung up across the world, leading thousands of people to God and to freedom from different specific addictions caused by the Disease. (Some of these are Alcoholics Anonymous, alcohol; Al-Anon, relationships; SAA, sex; EA, emotions; NA, narcotics; CA, cocaine; CoSa, relating to sex addicts; OA, overeating; FA, religious abuse; ABA, anorexic and bulimic disorders; CoDA, codependence.) The ambience of love and spiritual integrity in these groups is unlike anything I have seen. They have taken the tools of authentic faith that some of us had rejected, and God has created an incredible community of his people.

I am not trying to get the church to change and become something it is not—on the contrary. But I have tried to set out here the proposition that Sin is the addictive matrix out of which come the greed, the lust for power (and "to feel good"), and the numbing and self-defeating compulsions and addictions that cripple our best efforts and relationships and strangle our spiritual lives. And I have tried to point to the biblical tools and ways of living I have learned from people who love God and depend on him in a concrete way for their sanity and happiness. These are men and women whose lives have a serenity and integrity I want very much for my own.

If you try to live out the approach I have sketched here, I am convinced that God will guide you—through his Spirit and his Word—to find the particular shape your life should take. With regard to the mechanics of taking some of the steps recommended, you may want to talk to some people who are in one of the Twelve-Step programs like those I listed. They are fighting the same Disease, in some of its different manifestations, that we in the church are fighting as Sin.

A Worldwide Sickness

The present world situation is one in which the concept of Sin has been banished by many outside and inside the religious community. But the *same* Sin-disease we have been examining is permeating our society. A sense of miasma and depression is drifting like a fog across the land. Karl Menninger said over a decade ago that "no one is responsible" for the fouling of the air or the airwaves. We sit in the softness of our chairs and read about or watch child abuse, rape, social injustice, child pornography, and alcoholism going on all around us, with the constant overarching threat of nuclear war. Yet no one is responsible. We hear that neurotics need to be treated and criminals punished. And the rest of us sit around trying to find entertainment. As Menninger put it specifically,

> As it is, vague amorphous evil appears all about us, and this or that awful thing is happening. . . . and that wretched circumstance has developed, and yet, withal, when no one is responsible, no one is guilty, no moral questions are asked, when there is, in short, just nothing to do, we sink to despairing hopelessness. We wait from day to day for improvement, expectantly but not hopefully.[1]

But when the consciousness of Sin returns, hope returns. When we see our own self-centeredness and God-playing, we can begin to see it everywhere. We watch presidents, kings, and nations caught up—as we are—in the irrational blindness of their denial and grandiosity as they break the rules to get what they want. And when we see, we may be motivated to do something to change things in our lives and our world.

I believe that through the biblical message of the love and grace we have been given a "power of attorney" by God. We have been empowered to offer to the world the amazing news of his loving forgiveness for our Sin and the security of an eternal relationship with him that transcends death. But this relationship to God also provides for the here-and-now healing of the addictive Disease that subtly or openly moves to control the life of every person born into the world. This healing, and the serenity and joy that it brings are, I believe, the unique gift we who are surrendering our lives to God have to offer people everywhere.

But first I am convinced that each of us must begin dealing with Sin and denial in a very small and specific locale—within ourselves.

To contact J. Keith Miller regarding speaking engagements, write or call Michael McKinney, McKinney Associates, Inc., P.O. Box 5162, Louisville, KY 40205, (502) 583–8222.

Appendix

The Twelve Steps
(As adapted for this book)

1. We admitted we were powerless over our Sin—that our lives had become unmanageable.

2. Came to believe that a Power greater than ourselves could restore us to sanity.

3. Made a decision to turn our will and our lives over to the care of God as we understood God.

4. Made a searching and fearless moral inventory of ourselves.

5. Admitted to God, to ourselves, and to another human being the exact nature of our wrongs.

6. Were entirely ready to have God remove all these defects of character.

7. Humbly asked God to remove our shortcomings.

8. Made a list of all persons we had harmed, and became willing to make amends to them all.

9. Made direct amends to such people wherever possible, except when to do so would injure them or others.

10. Continued to take personal inventory and, when we were wrong, promptly admitted it.

11. Sought through prayer and meditation to improve our conscious contact with God, praying only for knowledge of God's will for us and the power to carry that out.

12. Having had a spiritual awakening as the result of these steps, we tried to carry this message to others and to practice these principles in all our affairs.

Reprinted with permission of Alcoholics anonymous World Services, Inc.:

The Twelve Steps as they appear in the Alcoholics Anonymous Big Book are (1) We admitted we were powerless over alcohol—that our lives had become unmanageable. (2) Came to believe that a Power greater than ourselves could restore us to sanity. (3) Made a decision to turn our will and our lives over to the care of God as we understood him. (4) Made a searching and fearless moral inventory of ourselves. (5) Admitted to God, to ourselves, and to another human being the exact nature of our wrongs. (6) Were entirely ready to have God remove all these defects of character. (7) Humbly asked him to remove our shortcomings. (8) Made a list of all persons we had harmed, and became willing to make amends to them all. (9) Made direct amends to such people wherever possible, except when to do so would injure them or others. (10) Continued to take personal inventory and, when we were wrong, promptly admitted it. (11) Sought through prayer and meditation to improve our conscious contact with God as we understood him, praying only for knowledge of his will and the power to carry that out. (12) Having had a spiritual awakening as the result of these steps, we tried to carry this message to alcoholics and to practice these principles in all our affairs.

Notes

CHAPTER 3

1. Karl Menninger, *Whatever Became of Sin?* (New York: Hawthorne, 1972), p. 25.
2. Marion J. Hatchett, *Commentary on the American Prayerbook* (San Francisco: Seabury Press, 1981), p. 449. See pp. 448–53, for an account of the development of penance, etc.
3. Through the rest of this book I will use a capital *S* for the word *sin* when it refers to that self-centered condition caused by putting oneself in the center where only God belongs. I will use the lower-case *s* when speaking of those harmful actions and thoughts that *result from* Sin.
4. William Temple, *Readings in St. John's Gospel* (London? Macmillan, 1963), p. 24.
5. Martin Luther, *Works*, Jaraslov Pelikan, ed. (St. Louis, MO: Concordia, 1955), vol. 36.
6. Hatchett, *Commentary*, p. 450.

CHAPTER 4

1. Karl Menninger, *Whatever Became of Sin?* (New York: Hawthorne, 1972). Many of the ideas in this chapter came from this book by Menninger.
2. Kenneth Scott Latourette, *A History of Christianity* (San Francisco: Harper—Row, 1953), pp. 657–59.
3. Menninger, *Whatever Became of Sin?* p. 24.
4. Arnold Toynbee, *Surviving the Future* (New York: Oxford University Press, 1971).

5. Mark Oraison, et al., *Sin*, trans. Bernard Murchland and Raymond Meyerpiter, with an introduction by Bernard Murchland (New York: Macmillan, 1962).

CHAPTER 5

1. L. J. Hatterer, *Encyclopedia of Psychology*, vol. 1, ed. Raymond J. Corsini (New York: Wiley, 1984), pp. 14, 15.
2. Harvey B. Milkman and Howard J. Shaffer, eds., *The Addictions: Multidisciplinary Perspectives and Treatment* (Lexington, MA: D.C. Heath, 1985), p. x.
3. Ibid., p. x.
4. Ibid.
5. Hatterer, *Encyclopedia of Psychology*, p. 14.
6. Ibid., p. 14.
7. Pia Mellody, with Andrea Wells Miller and J. Keith Miller, *Facing Codependence* (San Francisco: Harper & Row, 1989).

CHAPTER 6

1. The following sketch is based on interviews with counselees, Christian friends, and people in dozens of small groups over the past thirty years. The concepts of repression and denial as defenses of the ego were first described by Sigmund Freud. My attempt is to show how a defense mechanism can reinforce Sin until we have enough security in God to uncover it.
2. There is a "personal" quality about the Sin-disease that "feels like" dealing with a living adversary. Christians have traditionally spoken of the source of evil as Satan or "the tempter." But my own experience is that once I have accepted the bait, so to speak, and put myself in the center where only God belongs then *I* am responsible,

not Satan, and I must do battle with the Disease in me if I expect to recover.

3. Repression is a protective trick the mind plays on us by which it "sees" an unacceptable or very threatening feeling or thought coming. And just before the thought or feeling becomes *conscious* it is stuffed out of sight into our psychological basement. For example, a little boy being cross-examined by an angry father may "forget" that he did the thing he's being accused of—in the face of the impending wrath, punishment, and possible rejection of the father. (And so do we all.)

4. Besides repression and projection there are several other defenses against seeing our reality that the Sin-disease uses regularly to divert in harmful ways the energy attached to our denied feelings. Some of these are *reaction formation*: If I have a feeling that is too threatening for me to face, I may deny it and not be conscious of it. But "reaction formation" causes me to think that I have the *opposite* feeling. This can work two ways: if I hate people who are so strong and mean that they might kill me, reaction formation may cause me to think and act as though I really like them. Or if I love someone very much but am afraid he or she might reject me, I may deny my love and think and act as though I don't love that person at all. *Fixation and regression*: When I fail to move ahead in my emotional development because I am terrified I get *stuck* (and deny my fear); when I get terrified about something I can't face *now*, I *regress* to an earlier stage of emotional development and "hide" there. As an adult I may throw a tantrum as I did when I was a child.

   All these defenses (and others) against facing painful reality involve "denial" of conscious thoughts and feelings in different ways. (See Hall and Lindzey, *Theories of Personality* [New York: Wiley, 1957].)

5. Denial can be a healthy defense mechanism helping us

to block out shocks and grief that would destroy us if assimilated too quickly. But in healthy people the fog of denial passes gradually and the person experiencing the shock or grief can face it. The trouble comes when we deny anything that threatens our unnatural number-one position, which is rightly God's, and never see that we have denied this reality.

CHAPTER 7

1. Overeaters Anonymous has been an effective help to thousands who suffer from compulsive eating habits they cannot change. For information write to: Overeaters Anonymous, 2190 190th Street, Torrance, CA 90504 (213) 320–7941.
2. I am aware that the experiencing of overwhelming feelings, especially shame, is a major symptom of codependence, and that such feelings often come from abusive relationships in one's childhood. See Mellody, et al., *Facing Codependence*.
3. Although all of these behaviors do not indicate a serious problem of denial in everyone, I am describing the way I have behaved when denial has affected me.
4. E.g., see *The Doctor's Case Book in Light of the Bible, The Meaning of Persons*, and *Guilt and Grace* by Paul Tournier for good discussions on the effects of not being in touch with feelings and values.

CHAPTER 9

1. See *I'll Quit Tomorrow*, by Vernon E. Johnson (San Francisco: Harper & Row, 1980) for discussion of denial and delusion as experienced by an alcoholic.

CHAPTER 10

1. *Alcoholics Anonymous* (New York: Alcoholics Anonymous World Services, 1984), p. 61.

CHAPTER 11

1. You may recognize the steps described in this recovery process as having been adapted from the Twelve Steps of Alcoholics Anonymous and other programs dealing with specific compulsions and addictions manifested as a result of the Disease I am trying to describe here. For a complete list of the Twelve Steps as adapted for fighting the Sin-disease, see the Appendix. I strongly recommend studying these steps and taking them all to overcome the Sin-disease.
2. *Twelve Steps and Twelve Traditions* (New York: Alcoholics Anonymous World Services), p. 34.
3. Hobart Mowrer, *The Crisis in Psychiatry and Religion* (Princeton, NJ: Van Nostrand, 1961), pp. 54–55.

CHAPTER 12

1. There are a lot of tears in this story, and I feel self-conscious about showing them to you. But they came after a lifetime of mostly frozen feelings and are an important part of my recovery.

CHAPTER 14

1. Andrea Wells Miller, *BodyCare* (Waco, TX: Word Books, 1984).
2. I'm not talking here about helping people who are des-

titute or who have been crushed by society or circumstances. I believe we are sometimes called to help such people who cannot help themselves.

CHAPTER 16

1. Keith Miller's first three books, *The Taste of New Wine*, *A Second Touch*, and *Habitation of Dragons*, deal with trying to learn to live for God in various areas of ordinary life.
2. *Webster's 8th New Collegiate Dictionary* defines theology as "the study of God and his relation to the world, especially by analysis of the origins and teachings of an organized religious community (as the Christian Church)."
3. I realize as I'm writing this that I should pray this prayer before I read *anything*. But in fact I usually limit it to theology.

CHAPTER 17

1. The traditional word for this "turning" is *repentance* (in Greek: *metanoia*).
2. If you suspect you may have an addiction, for example to alcohol, drugs, food, sex, or gambling I strongly recommend going to an appropriate Twelve-Step group or a treatment center to check it out.
3. *Interpreter's Bible* (Nashville: Abingdon, 1952), vol. 12, p. 222.

CHAPTER 18

1. I was advised by Dr. Tournier that it is best to confess one on one in the presence of a minister or layperson who goes to confession him-or herself. But there are no rules about this.

CHAPTER 21

1. I am *not* saying that this kind of recovery group should engage in psychotherapy. In fact I believe they should *not* unless they have qualified leaders trained in group counseling. People with acute mental or emotional problems should be referred to professional therapists. But I am saying that remarkable and healing changes are routine in recovery groups (in which I've participated) made up of laypeople.

CHAPTER 23

1. Vernon E. Johnson, *I'll Quit Tomorrow* (San Francisco: Harper & Row, 1980), p. 48–61.

EPILOGUE

1. Menninger, *Whatever Became of Sin?* p. 188.

J. Keith Miller is a widely popular teacher, author, and speaker. He is the bestselling author of many books including *A Taste of New Wine*, *A Second Touch*, *Habitation of Dragons* and co-author of *Facing Codependence*. Currently he lives in Austin, Texas.